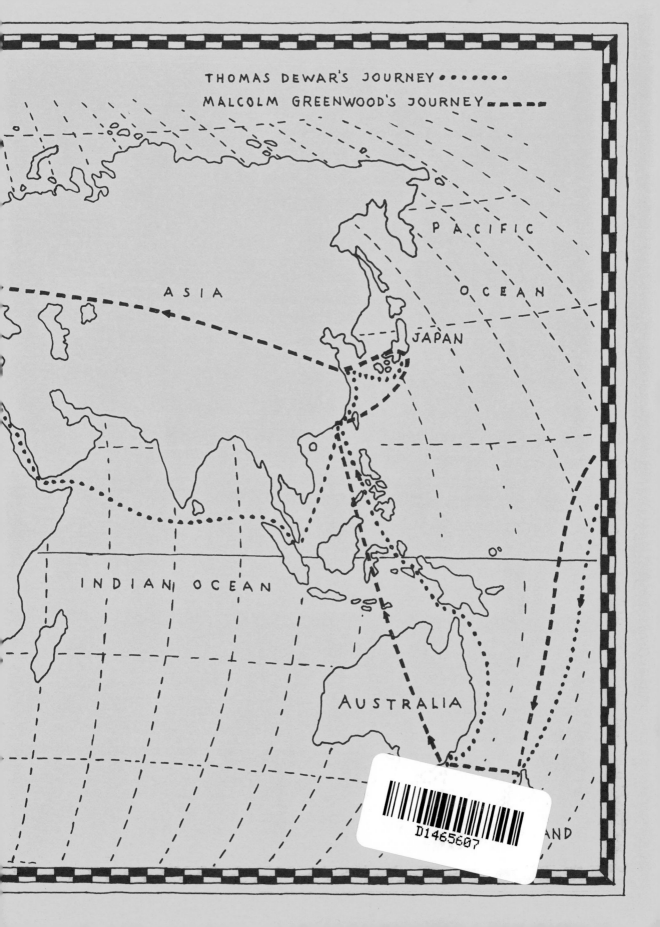

THOMAS DEWAR'S JOURNEY ••••••••
MALCOLM GREENWOOD'S JOURNEY━━━━━

PACIFIC

OCEAN

ASIA

JAPAN

INDIAN OCEAN

AUSTRALIA

0°

D1465607

AND

by Dewar's Responsibly.

's, and "White Label" are registered trademarks · ©1998 John Dewar's & Sons Company, Miami, FL · Blended Scotch Whisky · 40% ALC/VOL (80 Proof).

One does not solve the world's problems over a glass of white wine.

Dewar's®
scotch · whisky

Timeless Elegance

CRAIGELLACHIE HOTEL
of SPEYSIDE

A timeless presence in an everchanging world

Craigellachie Hotel of Speyside, Victoria Street, Craigellachie, Aberlour AB38 9SR
Telephone: 01340 881204   Fax: 01340 881253   www.craigellachie.com

The Speyside Cooperage and Visitor Centre

See the coopers at work using their traditional wood working tools as used in the "art of the cooper"

Established in 1947 by William Taylor, the Cooperage is still owned and run by the Taylor family. The Visitor Centre was added to the business in 1992 and since then the Company has received 13 awards for business initiatives, tourism, quality and efficiency. Visitors can watch the coopers at work from the safety of a viewing gallery and see an audio-visual presentation. There is a gift shop and refreshment facilities.

SPEYSIDE COOPERAGE · ACORN to CASK

SPEYSIDE COOPERAGE
CRAIGELLACHIE · BANFFSHIRE
SCOTLAND · AB38 9RS
TELEPHONE 01340 871108

1929.

Soup of the Day.

1999.

It was 70 years ago that Baxters produced their very first tin of Royal Game Soup. Its timeless quality has been enjoyed by generations of soup lovers ever since. That's because Baxters soups are produced with the very finest ingredients in the heart of Speyside. It doesn't matter what day it is, if it has a 'y' in it then it's a Baxters Royal Game Soup day.

Baxters. We've got a name for it.

A RAMBLE ROUND THE GLOBE REVISITED

Malcolm Greenwood

A RAMBLE ROUND THE GLOBE REVISITED

IN THE FOOTSTEPS
OF TOMMY DEWAR

Illustrated by Erik Foseid

NEIL WILSON PUBLISHING • GLASGOW • SCOTLAND

First published by

Neil Wilson Publishing

303a The Pentagon Centre

36 Washington Street

GLASGOW

G3 8AZ

Tel: 0141-221-1117

Fax: 0141-221-5363

E-mail: nwp@cqm.co.uk

http://www.nwp.co.uk/

© Malcolm Greenwood, 1999

Illustrations © Erik Foseid, 1999

The author has established his moral right to
be identified as the author of this work.

A catalogue record for this book is available
from the British Library.

ISBN 1-897784-96-1

Typeset in Bodoni

Designed by Mark Blackadder

Printed by WSOY, Finland

Also by the same author

A Nip Around The World (Argyll Publishing, 1995)

Another Nip Around The World (NWP, 1997)

CONTENTS

ACKNOWLEDGEMENTS

FIRST and foremost I would like to thank our sponsors who have been kind enough to take out advertising space at the front and rear of my book and without whose support this project would not have been possible. In attracting sponsorship, I was determined to approach companies that reflected the 'Dewar' spirit.

Many of these companies are Scottish, independent, family-run affairs, with a heritage which was formed over a hundred years ago, at the very time Tommy Dewar was forging the Dewar brand. Among them are Walkers of Aberlour (shortbread), Baxters of Fochabers (soups & preserves), Johnstons of Elgin (cashmere knitwear) and Gordon & MacPhail, also of Elgin, (whisky distillers). These companies are fiercely independent, maintaining exacting standards in quality, with strong export markets. Indeed, they are pioneers in the marketing of their wares. Their products could be seen in all of the countries I visited and this fact alone is a testament to their marketing skills. These markets are not easy options for exporters and are often crowded out by the 'big boys'. However, in general terms they are niche players and are small enough to be flexible and react quickly to changing demand, easier to deal with than the anonymous multinationals, and above all, you can depend on them.

Highland Spring and The Speyside Cooperage are companies which have been formed in more recent times: 1979 and 1947 respectively, yet display the characteristics Tom would have admired. These are attention to high quality, marketing drive, innovation, and an unwavering faith and confidence in their products.

The Craigellachie Hotel, now over 100 years old, epitomises the style and grace of a bygone era. This hotel offers a warm welcoming atmosphere with unobtrusive, yet professional and attentive service. Tom, I am sure, would have loved the 'Quaich Bar' with one of the largest selections of malt whiskies in the world – over 300 bottlings!

Lastly John Dewar & Sons who have carried Tom's 'spirit' into the next century. They have most graciously allowed me to reproduce Nicholas Morgan's history of the company which was first published on the 150th anniversary of the company's founding. John Dewar & Sons have won the

Queen's Award for Export Achievement on six separate occasions. This is a testament to the company's contribution to Britain's exports to the rest of the world and reflects the continuing success of Dewar's, built on the pioneering efforts of Tommy Dewar. This is particularly evident in the United States, Tommy Dewar's first, and most favourite, overseas market.

I am indebted to the following individuals whom I wish to thank.

AUSTRALIA
Nina Mavris, Sydney Hilton

CANADA
Philip Groulx, Ottawa
Ian and John Hanna, Toronto

CHINA
Lisa Leung, Jane Dong & Zhang Hai Ling, Shanghai Hilton

ENGLAND
Sukhindar Singh, London
Rudy Jagersbacker, London Hilton

NEW ZEALAND
Maggie Barretta, Fred Grover and Dawn Hughes, Auckland

USA
Lola Preiss, New York Hilton
Lesley Silbertstein, Back Bay Hilton, Boston
Jo Ann Bongiorno, Chicago Hilton
Catherine Franklin, Washington Hilton
Deborah Larkin, San Francisco Hilton
Bernie Caalim-Palanzi, Hawaii Hilton
Bill Burke & Chris Hawkes, Boston, Massachusetts
Tom Ovens, Los Gatos, California
John & Shelagh Greenwood, Richmond, Virginia
Gordon Christopherson, Alameda, California

SCOTLAND
Neil Boyd, John Dewar & Sons, Glasgow
Sue Beaton & Karen Wilson, Beaver Travel, Forres
Linda McAdam, Forres
Bissett & Taylor, Elgin
Douglas Ashmead, Jim McDowell, Mike Dewar, Trevor Potts, Andy McBean, Janet Gray, Dr Jackie Mobbs, Charles Smith, Barrie Chown, John Nicholson and Gordon Webster, all from Elgin
Norman Shepherd & Alan Mearns, Aberdeen

INTRODUCTION

THE idea to write this book surfaced quite by chance. It took no effort, no grand plan, it simply arrived through my office door. It was 1995 and the late-afternoon darkness of winter filled my office with melancholy. I was sitting at my desk at Glenfarclas Distillery on the banks of the River Spey when in breezed our sprightly chairman George Grant; at 78 years of age still involved with the running of this world-famous family-owned business. 'Pleased to read your first book Malcolm – great idea,' he remarked.

He was referring to the diary of a whisky salesman, yours truly, which had just been published as *A Nip Around The World*. The contents were mostly humorous tales of my travels abroad in search of new whisky markets. His comment was pleasing and I felt honoured. He then proceeded to lay down a very worn and dog-eared book on my desk. It looked at least a century old, and on further inspection I found that it was. When I had been trying to think of a title for my book, I had gone through over 50 possibilities before selecting *A Nip Around The World*. I gaped in astonishment at the musty edition in my hand…*A Ramble Round The Globe* by Tommy Dewar. This was the first time that I had heard of the book and the coincidence fascinated me.

I read the whole book that evening, completely engrossed. It was a travel memoir full of the observations of the Victorian whisky baron Sir Thomas Dewar on one of his many sales trips around the world in the late 1890's. This was the beginning of Dewar's dominance in the American market, where, to this day, it is still the brand leader amongst blended whiskies. His sales trip took place in the age of sail and steamships, horse-drawn carriages, Pullman railway coaches, the gold standard, telegrams, private hotels, quack medicine and the British Empire. Compare all that to what we know today: jumbo jets, TGV trains, Eurodollars, E-mail, the Internet, international hotel chains, genetic cloning, and a devolved Scotland.

As I contemplated the world that Dewar must have witnessed I realised that I simply had to retrace Tommy's trail and compare my world with the one in his book. I might as well say this now, to save you a lot of trouble, I will refer to the 'Dewar' character as Tom. He was widely known, after all, as 'Whisky Tom'.

As Tom's book went to print the world was about to change dramatically: Britain had just been involved in a guerrilla war in Boer South Africa and Europe was gradually drifting towards the first of two world wars which would alter Western society for ever. No-one, Tom included, could have imagined the rise of the superpowers, both political and corporate. Yet, I wondered, has the world changed so very much? And if so, is it for the better?

I felt a bit envious of Tom's leisurely journeying. How civilised the pace was then. But I reminded myself that only a very small minority in Tom's day had the means or opportunity to travel, let alone internationally. How did Tom manage all this? After all, he had spent the early years of his business life in Leith and Perth.

With these thoughts in mind I set about planning my trip and ensured that I diaried a window of six weeks over the Christmas and New Year period at the end of 1998. The prospect enthralled me. America, Canada, Hawaii, Fiji, New Zealand, Australia, China, and Hong Kong were all on my itinerary. But six weeks! How would I cope? Well, if Tom could do it, then so could I.

Finally, on the subject of travel, always remember that it contains a threatening element of gambling, of dicing with life itself. It is, ultimately, one of the most exciting experiences anyone can undertake. I hope you enjoy the world that Tom knew and the one that I found.

MALCOLM GREENWOOD
Elgin, July 1999

CHAPTER 1

THE TOMMY DEWAR STORY BY DR NICHOLAS MORGAN

*First published in 1996 on the 150th anniversary
of the foundation of John Dewar & Sons*

1996 marks the celebration of the 150th anniversary of the foundation of John Dewar & Sons, creators of Dewar's White Label, one of the world's largest selling Scotch whisky brands and America's favourite blend. This anniversary is an almost unique achievement, not only in the world of Scotch whisky, where few firms can claim such a sustained history as blenders, brand owners and market leaders as Dewar's, but also in the world of business as a whole, where a lifespan of 150 years is remarkable. Few other popular brands, whether spirits, soft drinks or soap, can claim such a sustained heritage as Dewar's: none can pretend to the same timelessness, quality and spiritedness that characterises Dewar's first 150 years.

John Dewar was born near Aberfeldy in Perthshire in 1806. He was born on a relatively large and prosperous farm and was one of a large family. Educated at the local parish school, where the learning would have been of a standard much admired today, he subsequently (1821) apprenticed to a joiner in the nearby village of Weem. Five years later, the apprenticeship complete, John moved to Aberfeldy where he joined brother James as a partner in the latter's joinery business. Within two years however he embarked on a major career change moving to the city of Perth where he joined his uncle James MacDonald as a cellarman in his wine and spirit business. Quickly learning the basics of the business John was offered a partnership in the firm following James MacDonald's death in 1837. He remained a partner there until 1846 when he branched out in business on his own account and established a firm of wine and spirit merchants in Perth's High Street.

1846 was a propitious time to begin such a business, as John must have realised. Perth, until recently Scotland's second city, was nonetheless growing at a considerable rate. No longer just a country town serving outlying agricultural districts, it boasted a range of new industries, such as linen manufacture and dyeing. Traditional services and markets and new industries combined to make Perth a centre of industry and commerce, providing new employment opportunities for workers attracted from the countryside, where continuing improvements in agriculture were forcing labourers from the land. New relationships were being forged based on wages, contracts and commercial transactions, as opposed to traditional forms of payment in kind. And new urban markets were being formed of people who in the past might have baked their own bread, brewed their own beer, and possibly distilled their own whisky; now, living in towns, they were dependent on merchants and grocers like John Dewar to provide for their needs.

Scotch whisky, at the time that John Dewar started his business, was still held in low esteem by the sort of discerning and well-to-do clients that he was trying to attract. Distilling in the Highlands was emerging from the shadow of illicit manufacture. Production of malt whisky was still on a relatively small scale, and quality, except from a few well-established and well known distilleries, was variable. In the Lowlands, whisky was distilled from both malted and unmalted grains, in large shallow stills that enabled distillers to produce spirit quickly, and in quite large quantities, but very often only of a poor character. The Coffey still, which enabled these Lowland distillers to produce a high quality grain spirit without the unpleasant burnt flavour that characterised their existing product, was just about to be perfected.

John Dewar was well poised to take advantage of these changes in the 1840s and it was probably an awareness of the opportunities that whisky seemed to offer that encouraged him to set up his business. His training in the MacDonald's cellars had taught him the basic skills of blending, and how much could be achieved by mixing together complimentary components in order to produce a final blend that was far better than the sum of its constituent parts. So John set about blending whiskies, working from a limited range of malts, (mainly from the eastern Highlands and what we now call Speyside) and grains, to impose his quality standards on his whisky in order to produce a drink that was suitable to the palates of those more accustomed to drinking fine wines and brandies. Having dealt in such products for nearly 20 years he was well aware of the competition he faced. He also knew that he needed to produce whisky that was distinctively his, better than those produced by other grocers in Perth, such as his neighbour and rival Arthur Bell, to ensure that customers would come back to buy it again, asking for Dewar's whisky by name, differentiating it from competitors. So in this environment not only the first blends, but the first brands, were born.

John Dewar's business was small but successful. By 1860 he had employed his first traveller to try and expand his business beyond the immediate confines of Perth and in 1869 he added a second. Two years later his eldest son John A Dewar joined the business, becoming a partner in 1879 at the age of 23; by this time John the elder was partially retired and was perhaps already suffering from the ill-health that was to bring about his death in January of the following year, aged 74. John the younger took over the firm and brought into it his youngest brother Thomas (or Tommy), who had received some training in the 'whisky business' capital of Leith. By 1885 Tommy was a partner.

The brothers had clear ambitions to expand the range of their father's modest business and their success was remarkable, even by the standards of the day. When John inherited the firm the capital was less than £10,000 and profits stood at only £1,321. In 1894 the brothers converted the business to a private company with a capital of £100,000 and the profits stood at nearly £20,000. In 1897 Dewar's became a public company with capital of £600,000; by 1900 annual profits stood at £59,000. By 1925 the firm's annual profits were in excess of £1 million. When John Dewar died in 1929 he left an estate of over £4.5 million; Tommy died less than twelve months later leaving over £5 million. These prodigious numbers shine only the slightest light on the genius and spirit that underpinned Dewar's triumph.

Risk (personal and financial), steadfastness, innovation and an unmoveable commitment to quality all contributed to the company's success, but at its heart lay the character, spirit and energy of John and Tommy, diverse personalities united in their unswerving commitment to the success of Dewar's.

Their first move was to expand the range of blends they produced and they also began to brand them more clearly and uniformly, at this time under the name of Dewar's Perth Whisky. But markets needed to grow as well as the product range; a few agencies had been appointed by John when he first joined the business, but it was Tommy's drive that expanded the horizons of the business. In 1885, aged only 21, he moved to London in order to open up the trade there. Whisky was still a relatively new drink; Tommy's objective was to recruit both a suspicious trade and non-whisky literate customers to both the category and more importantly, the Dewar's brand. He began with only two business contacts; one turned out to be dead and the other bankrupt. Nonetheless the firm's small London offices were soon flourishing. Tommy's methods were partly traditional. He would cold-call wholesalers and retailers again and again with samples trying to persuade them to stock Dewar's brands on the basis of taste and quality until orders gradually began to arrive. However he also adopted a grander strategy in order to bring Dewar's name before the public. One was to exhibit Dewar's at the many national and trade exhibitions that were held throughout the United Kingdom. In 1886 Dewar's won their first of over 50 medals at the Edinburgh International Exhibition in a competitive tasting against the major whisky brands of the day. Dewar's has since graced the prize winners at exhibitions as diverse as Edinburgh, Antwerp, Paris, Brussels, London, Chicago, St Louis, Salonika, Buenos Aires and Cairo. No other whisky has won more medals than Dewar's.

Exhibitions were often difficult ground for small firms to tread; for Tommy they offered an opportunity to exercise some of his more audacious stunts. Isolated on a remote stall at a Brewer's exhibition in Birmingham with no passing custom, Tommy employed a piper in full Highland dress to stand at the Dewar's stall and play as loudly as he could. Pretty soon the power of the pipes in a confined place worked to Tommy's advantage;

hordes of visitors clamoured around the Dewar's stall to see where the noise was coming from whilst competitors raged, demanding that the piper should be stopped. Tommy politely refused, having learnt a lesson in marketing that he would never forget. As they gained experience in exhibiting so their stands became more elaborate; brightly painted and gaily lit, very often policed by kilted brand ambassadors encouraging visitors to sample Dewar's. Novelty was, typically for Dewar's, also important; the Dewar's stand at the Glasgow 1901 International Exhibition, in addition to housing 'interesting curios relating to the firm' featured a 'Mutoscopic' reproduction of *The Whisky of His Ancestors* painting, in which the characters were brought alive before the eyes of the audience.

The move to London brought a considerable increase in business; in 1888 Tommy Dewar had obtained the contract as sole supplier of Scotch whisky to the London caterers Spiers and Pond following a tasting against a range of competitors blends. Their outlets varied from railway station buffets, through restaurants and hotels to music halls. The orders were large, frequent and increasing. To keep up with this demand changes were required in Perth. The general offices were expanded and additional bonded premises acquired. In 1890, in order to ensure supplies of whisky, Dewar's took out a long lease on Tullymet Distillery in Perthshire and also entered into a long-term credit arrangement with the Distiller's Company for the supply of grain whisky. In the following year the word 'Dewar' was registered as a trademark. In 1893, partly as a result of Tommy Dewar's efforts in spreading the word about Dewar's in London, the company was awarded a Royal Warrant by Queen Victoria which has been renewed by successive monarchs. Royal Warrants were also later granted by Alfonso XIII, King of Spain in 1907 and by the King of Sweden, and the German Kaiser in 1909.

Staff were also required; naturally enough the two brothers chose young men of their own generation with a similar outlook on the world to join the business. They stayed, and became the backbone of Dewar's success. In London Tommy had recruited Fred Whitefield as an office boy. He inherited the London business at a stroke when Tommy began his world travels. He later became a director. In 1890 both A J Cameron, the creator of white Label, and Peter M Dewar, who was to inherit Tommy Dewar's mantle as the Dewar world traveller, both joined the firm that they were to remain with throughout their careers. Branches were also established throughout the United Kingdom in the late 1890s with managers who similarly stayed, and made, Dewar's.

After over five years of hard work in London, Tommy Dewar had successfully established Dewar's whisky as one of the leading brands in the Metropolis. He was already a well-known figure in the Capital, famous for his whisky and wit, and embarking on the first steps of his political career where his trenchant and anti-temperance and anti-taxation views made frequent newspaper headlines. However he needed a larger stage on which to promote Dewar's and to satisfy his sense of adventure and vanity. So in August 1892 he set out on the first of his two world tours, which, after his later journey of 1898, he subsequently narrated in a book, *A Ramble Round The Globe*. Setting out only armed with a small quantity of samples Tommy Dewar visited 26 countries, and appointed 32 agents for Dewar's in two years of travelling. The cost of the first expedition was £14,000. Whisky was a relatively well established drink in many overseas markets by this time, particularly throughout the British Empire. Typically, Tommy did not follow in the well-trodden path of other whisky salesmen, but rather he turned his head towards the United States, at this time a relatively small market for Scotch, but one where Dewar's had already made an impact. In 1891 Andrew Carnegie, the Scottish-born magnate whose millions had been earned in the steel business in the United States, ordered a 'small keg' of whisky from Dewar's to be sent to Benjamin Harrison, then President of the United States. When the cask was duly delivered it caused an uproar, not least because reporters seized on the event as showing Harrison's failure to support home-grown products. It was political fuss with wide repercussions, as Tommy was to recall:

'There was hardly a newspaper in America which had not obtained details of the offending cask, the result being that inquiries and orders flowed to us from all parts of the States.'

This, he claimed, 'was the very best advertisement I ever had', and 'certainly the cheapest.' It meant that when he arrived in New York he had little difficulty in appointing the firm's first agent there, who subsequently opened a Dewar's brand office in Bleeker Street. When he visited the White House on his travels (as a tourist) he was also able to tell the guide that there was at least one Scottish product in its cellars!

Tommy Dewar's arrival in New York marked the start of a love affair that was to remain with him for the rest of his life. 'My first impressions of New York were that it was a wonderful place,' he later wrote, and this sense of wonderment with America, and particularly New York, never left him. He was to become, along with close friends such as Thomas Lipton, the genius behind the growth of multiple retailing, New York's favourite Scotsman, as feted and newsworthy there as he was in London. He also embarked on a lifelong lust for travel and the adventure it brought with it. In addition to the United States he had taken in countries such as New Zealand, Australia, Hong Kong, mainland China, Japan and Egypt during his first journey. He undertook his second world sales tour before the end of the century and, in addition to his frequent travels to the United States, travelled widely in Europe and Africa. Everywhere he went the newspapers followed. When he travelled to East Africa in 1913 for a big-game hunting expedition he ensured that his exploits were recorded on camera for later publication in national newspapers.

The impact of Tommy Dewar's successful bid to expand the company's overseas business was enormous. Almost overnight the scale of the concern was transformed; turnover and profits rocketed. It was John Dewar who managed this growth, putting in place the infrastructure and logistics that were needed to meet the demand that his brother had stimulated. In order to secure supplies of malt whiskies for blending John had first acquired Tullymet Distillery in Perthshire in 1890. In 1896 the firm feud ground at Aberfeldy and built a model distillery there to John Dewar's design which was opened in 1898. Subsequently, distillery acquisitions included Lochnagar in 1922 and Aultmore on Speyside, and Ord on the Black Isle in 1923. There were also massive expansions in the blending and bottling operations in Perth which were completed with the opening of the East Bond in the city in 1912. By this time the work that A J Cameron had begun in the blending room was complete. Cameron had developed a new method of blending techniques which involved pre-vatting malt whiskies by region of origin and also pre-vatting grains, leaving the vats to mature until the exact moment was reached for the final blending process. The signature of the eastern Highlands, that had marked the first Dewar's blends, was retained by Cameron in his blend with Aberfeldy, the sweet and heathery malt whisky that John and Tommy Dewar had made for themselves in order to capture the very essence of their blending tradition and retain it's distinctive regionality. The blend, named simply White Label, proudly displaying the Dewar exhibition medals and their Royal Warrant, was introduced onto the market in 1906.

Having built a network of distributors for the brand around the world the company were faced with developing and maintaining a presence for the brand in the eyes of the public. It was here that Tommy's genius was to shine most brightly. He was a natural exponent of the art of advertising and the spirit of his earlier stunts was to be carried through into Dewar's advertising and point-of-sale which was probably the most outstanding of the time. Advertising, for Tommy, had to be 'bold and attractive – let the picture on the hoarding', he said, 'be so attractive that the people will miss their train.' He also took a sophisticated and global view of advertising. 'It is important to catch the eye of the travelled public to impress them as they pass through the great centres like London, Paris and New York: they pass along and create business for you in all parts of the world.'

No technique was ignored. In 1898 he commissioned the first film advertisement for a drinks company. Made by the Edison Company, the film featured characters acting out *The Whisky of his Forefathers* painting that the firm was to use so widely in their press and poster advertising, coming to life, dancing and toasting Dewar's. It was first shown on a large screen on the roof of the Pepper Building in New York's Herald Square. This use of film was continued when in 1927 Dewar's made one of the first documentaries on the production of Scotch whisky. In 1911 they erected 'the largest mechanical sign in Europe', a massive neon Scotsman on the London Embankment whose hand, holding a glass of Dewar's, moved up and down from his mouth. The sign caused astonishment, amusement and outrage and in keeping with Tommy Dewar's principles, brought homeward bound commuters to a halt.

Dewar's had also begun advertising in the press before most of their competitors, employing wit, sometimes outrageously absurd historical allusions, striking graphical design and topical references to promote their brand. Early advertising was designed to persuade consumers of the purity and the age of the product, consistency was also an important message, with the strapline, 'it never varies' quickly becoming attached to the brand. Tommy Dewar also exploited colour advertising long before many of their competitors. His adverts were carefully designed to attract a range of age groups to the product, continuing the recruitment efforts that had marked his early career. Many exploited works of art that Tommy had bought specifically for the purpose of advertising. 'In my opinion the medium for advertising should always be high class – a cheap style denotes a cheap article.' The tone of the advertising that his early work set was continued after the death of John and Tommy Dewar. The benchmark was quality, and not just of course, of the advertising. The article, wrote Tommy, 'is its own best advertiser, the quality must always be a convincing testimonial that it is the best that money can buy.'

Between them the two Dewar brothers had created one of the world's largest whisky brands; by 1920 they were neck and neck for supremacy with Buchanan's and Walker's. The two men who had taken over a modest business in Perth and transformed it so dramatically, had prospered in the process. John Dewar was one of the most prominent Scotsmen of his day; he was a philanthropist in the city of Perth and its county without compare, a leading Liberal politician who was knighted in 1907 and elevated to the peerage as Lord Forteviot (a title which continues today) in 1917. He had purchased the large estate and castle at Dupplin, near Perth in 1910 which was to become, and remain the Dewar home. In 1907, his son also John, entered the business, a family tradition which has been continued up to the current Lord Forteviot, who joined the business as a trainee and served in all its branches before becoming a director, eventually retiring from his executive role in 1977.

Tommy Dewar, largely by design, had become one of the most famous and talked-about men of his generation. He was knighted in 1902 and became Lord Dewar in 1919; he held various offices in the City of London and was also a Conservative MP. He was a friend of the stars, counting among his acquaintances performers such as Harry Lauder (another Scot who was taken to the hearts of New Yorkers) and Dan Leno. He was a close friend of Gordon Selfridge, the retailing magnate from Chicago who came to London determined to build the world's greatest department store. Selfridge, like Tommy Dewar and Thomas Lipton, was an outstanding pioneer in the art of understanding and communicating with his customer, in a way that both informed and exhilarated. But it was Lipton who was Tommy Dewar's closest friend. They were known as the two most famous bachelors of their day, and like current-day celebrities, lived much of their private lives in public. Their yachting exploits and practical joking were almost as newsworthy as the 'Dewarisms' for which Tommy Dewar became renowned. As a public speaker he was in enormous demand; his speeches and travels were widely reported: 'We have a great regard for old age when it is bottled,' or 'Advertising is to business what imagination is to poetry,' are just two examples of the jokes that made the headlines – pithy, and sometimes strikingly irreverent for the times. ('Respectability is the state of never being caught doing anything which gives you pleasure.') These 'Dewarisms' captured the spiritedness, and the sheer sense of fun and enjoyment, that was and is Dewar's, and underpinned some of the forward-thinking views that marked out the brand from its competitors.

The two brothers died within twelve months of each other but the trajectory they had established for their business was remorseless. Well established throughout the world with an early foothold in the United States, Dewar's was well positioned to grow rapidly after the repeal of probation in the USA in 1933, and again after the end of the dislocations of the Second World War in 1945. The export achievements of the firm were celebrated by six Queen's Awards for Export Achievement between 1966 and 1984. During that time Dewar's had captured over 15% of Scotch whisky sales in the United States, giving it a position of dominance in that market which it retains today. However, the pioneering travels of Tommy Dewar and his successors had also created other markets, such as Greece, Spain, the Lebanon and Venezuela which remain core Dewar's markets today. In all of these markets Dewar's still retains the reputation for quality that was the essential element that assured its early successes; however, the brand also exhibits a fiercely independent and innovative approach to its marketing that reflects the spiritedness of Tommy Dewar. Together, these timeless core values ensure that Dewar's is celebrating its 150th anniversary with as much, if not more, thought for the future than it is giving to the past, *writes Dr Nicholas Morgan.*

*   *   *

IN late 1898, Tom embarked on a journey which would, over a period of two years, take him around the world. It was no mean feat in those days and subject to many physical dangers; modern medicine as we know it simply did not exist. He was, however, privileged for his time. Only the very rich and the armed forces travelled so extensively. His trip was to set him back over half a million pounds in today's terms* (around £14,000 then) whilst my costs for covering this journey would amount to £3,000. This point alone, highlights just how affordable travelling abroad is today. My trip would take a considerably shorter time; six weeks in all. It started on 15 December 1998, one hundred years after Tom's.

As previously mentioned, when Tom returned from his journey he

* Source: Bank of Scotland

published his experiences in his book *A Ramble Round The Globe* and I will be including extracts from this in order to compare and contrast the world he travelled through with my own observations a century later. Any text attributed to Tom will be accompanied in the margin with Erik's rendition of Tom's visage. My own text is similarly accompanied, but you will have no difficulty in discerning between us! Let us begin at the beginning. What follows are Tom's introductory passages from *A Ramble Round The Globe*.

TD

In offering this book to the public, I should like it to be distinctly understood that I do not claim for it any particular literary merit, neither do I wish it to be thought I intend entering the ranks of the noble army of authors. It is simply the gratification of a fad. After I had finished my tour, so many of my friends wanted to know 'all about it,' that I determined to fill up my odd time by putting it down on paper; and this is the result. Some of the little tales recorded may be new, or they may have reached an age when they may justly be termed 'bald-headed'; whichever they are, I do not claim originality for them. I simply record them as they come to me. There is a quotation somewhere that would come in most aptly at the beginning of this book, if I could only find it, so as to put it down correctly. As far as my memory serves me, it is something about great events springing up from little causes; and I should like to use it, as it was a very little cause that brought about the publication of this book. It was a cold, and there is no doubt about that being a very little cause. We all know that a cold is the start of a good many things, but it seems funny that it should be the start of a book; still, such was the case in this instance.

It happened this way. When fighting for the 'Moderate' cause in West Marylebone for a seat in the London County Council, against representatives of the Church and the Bar, and amidst all the delights of blinding blizzards, east winds, and snow-storms, as well as my seat I caught a cold. I could have done without the cold, had I been consulted on the matter; but I wasn't, so I had to put up with it.

That cold was evidently possessed of an inquisitive and exploring nature, for it was very restless. First it settled in one part, then went to another, then had a general tour round; till at last the grave and serious-looking medical gentleman who had been endeavouring for some time to 'fix' it looked graver and still more serious. Warmer climes were ordered. Now, it is not a very difficult matter to find a warmer climate than the one 'made for Great Britain'; but when a choice has to be made, the worry of selection becomes objectionable, so, just to save this worry, I decided to sample the lot and go round the world. Hence it arises that a simple cold became the little cause from which sprang the great event of my foreign travel and subsequent publication of this book.

THOMAS R DEWAR
London, October 1904

MG

This book is the simple gratification of my travel bug. My tales will simply be recorded as they happen. If I don't like something I will say so. What caused me great amusement prior to my departure, was that I, like Tom, had a cold. It is a trifle ironic that our dear virus friends steadfastly endure through the centuries. I read recently that the common cold is indeed incurable; made up from countless and changing viruses causing misery the world over. In an average lifespan we will spend three years of our lives with the cold. In this respect little has changed since Tom's days. But I did have something, literally up my sleeve, which Tom would not have contemplated: I had been inoculated!

TD

The procuring of the necessary outfit for a journey through all parts of the globe is an awful bother; and then, when it has been got together, there is the packing. The plagues of Egypt may have been bad, but such an awful ordeal as superintending this packing, without doubt, eclipses the lot! It was done at last, though, and then a start was made.

MG

It is indeed a bother, but I am sure, given my shorter journey time, that it is now much less of a bother. Your suitcases would have been heavy trunks or portmanteau; mine would out of necessity be light and easily carried. One of my cases was a canvas backpack and the other a small wheely case. A shoulder bag with all my documents, money, credit cards etc, I carried on my person all the time. At a stretch this baggage was in most instances termed 'Hand Luggage' which reduced the risk of temporary loss with airline baggage handling. This was important to me, as it would have been extremely difficult for the different airlines to catch up with me on a constantly changing address. Travelling light was the key.

TD

Determining to travel with the sun, and begin with 'The West, to the West the land of the free,' the actual starting-point was Euston Station; and this I left amidst farewells from friends. Liverpool was reached without incident, and I was soon located on board a great Atlantic liner, ready to make a real start. That starting is a terrible business. The last tender arrives, passengers and friends come on board, the luggage and mails are transferred, out clangs the bell announcing that friends must leave the ship, as the tender is ready to depart; and then comes the affecting time. Good-bye has to be said, the time for parting has arrived; and many who have been talking together with forced gaiety, or standing silent in sadness, now utterly break down. Still it has to be done; and, heedless of the indescribable sorrow experienced by many hundreds on board, the bell still clangs out, and the warning cry, 'All for the shore,' still goes on. At last the gangway is up, the tender moves one way, and we move in the other direction, and with a sea of handkerchiefs waving from both, the one boat goes back to the wharf, while the other goes forward to face the perils and dangers of the Atlantic. The SS *Paris* is a grand ship. No care nor trouble was spared in her construction, the great idea being that, as far as human foresight could provide, she should be absolutely unsinkable, and the next, that she should be able to go at not less than 20 knots per hour throughout the voyage. She has a length of 560 feet, a beam of 63 feet, a depth of 43 feet and has a 10,498 tonnage. Nearly 300 tons of coal are used every day while the vessel is at sea...about one ton every five minutes. I must say the arrangements on board are almost perfect, if not quite so; and if it were not for the eccentric behaviour of the ocean upon occasions, the luxury and comfort would be unequalled by even the best hotels in England.

MG

My departure on 15 December 1998 was without fuss. Nothing romantic or sad in the least. My last night with two close friends was memorable and caused me, on this rare occasion, to sleep in. Janet just laughed. 'Jesus Christ! Off round the world and you sleep in!'

My friend Jim arrived on time to take me to Aberdeen Airport. Thankfully all my light luggage had been packed the night before. I ached a bit from the recent inoculations: typhoid, polio, hepatitis A and tetanus.

It was a beautiful crisp and blue-skied day en route to Aberdeen. My first flight today would be short and sweet to London Heathrow aboard a British Airways Boeing 727 named *Robert Louis Stevenson*. I did not realise then that I would cross RLS's tracks on this trip. I settled back as the aircraft accelerated along a breeze-swept runway. Most of this journey would be by plane and would take me six weeks to complete my own ramble round the globe.

I arrived at Heathrow at around midday with a short connection before boarding another BA flight bound to JFK New York. This was a another Boeing, a 747/100 flown by Captain Steve Buzdygan. This marvellous machine has shrunk the world to an extent that Tom could never have imagined. This airliner carries 356 people, and at the time of writing much larger aircraft capable of carrying 500 passengers are in the pipeline. The flight-time of around $6\frac{1}{2}$ hours compared to Tom's voyage of 6 days. If my budget had been larger I could have flown supersonic on Concorde with a journey time of less than three hours. That's less than the running time of the movie Titanic. On this topic, Tom's surroundings on board would have been similar to that portrayed in the film.

The aircraft was carrying 201 passengers out of a possible 356. The best option on a half-full 747 is the central rows of four seats. That way the armrests can be folded up and you make a reasonable bed. In fact, this option, if you can get it, can be preferable to business class. To protect your bed from 'predators' you have firstly to assume your position in the second seat in from the aisle. Once this is achieved you quickly spread out magazines, books, CDs etc into the adjacent seats. This reduces the risk of losing your bed. Finally, if a predator starts to eye up your 'park bench'

you either give him or her a filthy stare, or blow them a kiss, depending on how you regard them. This is the life of a hobo on a jumbo!

It still remains a mystery to me how this squat, fat aircraft does the job. But what a job it does. The cabin lights were dimmed, the engines droned on. The flight chart on the screen indicated we were 35,000 feet up and travelling at 512 mph. This aircraft would burn 10,200 kg of fuel per hour, requiring 81,600 kg for the entire journey. The total weight on lift-off was 289,500 kg.

Dinner had passed with some pleasant wine; and a press of the button on the armrest brought a smiling hostess offering a night-cap. I tried to relax and wondered what Tom would have thought of this technological marvel. I downed the last of my malt whisky and thought of one of Tom's Dewarisms.

'A philosopher is a man who can look at an empty glass with a smile.'

*   *   *

NEW YORK

TD

On the Wednesday following the one on which we left Liverpool there was great excitement on board, for we were close in to New York; and to those who, like myself, were going to get their first sight of that wonderful place, the time was particularly interesting. The young American lady whom I had befriended early in the voyage repaid my gallantry by pointing out all the places of interest. She pointed out New Jersey and I timidly inquired what it might be famous for, and got the reply, 'Mosquitos'. I found out afterwards that the young lady was right. Certainly the approach to New York is a very fine view; the great Statue of Liberty, standing well out as it does, seems to give a welcome to all who are approaching that great and marvellous country – America. As we gradually drew near land, the enthusiasm of the American portion of passengers grew more intense, and almost wild excitement glared from every eye. Suddenly, without seemingly any warning, there burst out from the shore and on board a waving of miniature 'Stars and Stripes'. Almost everybody seemed provided with these little flags, and they waved them wildly and excitedly, with a vigour almost bordering on frenzy. Naturally, they had all advised their friends beforehand – hence the enthusiasm; but as the stolid Britisher does not care to advertise himself so much, this display is never seen on our shores. I really think that the Custom-house business could be done much quicker. However, it does not do to say anything, as Custom-house officers have an awkward knack of making things disagreeable, as I saw in one case. An American girl next to me, who was having her baggage examined, cheeked the officer more than he cared for; so, opening a huge trunk, he carefully slid his hands down the sides to the bottom, and in bringing them up turned the whole of the contents topsy-turvy. My! I never saw such a lot of ladies under-garments before, not even in a shop window. The frilled arrangements and peculiar articles that seemed all fluff and lace, frocks and frills, embroidered hose and silk – ahem! were all exposed to view, and the poor girl had to repack the lot. I felt very sorry for her, and would have helped, but thought I had better not, as, not being used to such garments, I might fold them up wrongly.

MG

Although much swifter than Tom's journey I could not help but think how clinical it all was. There is not much opportunity to socialise on transatlantic flights; the dreaded in-flight movie tends to deny this opportunity. Even if you do not wish to watch it, you are obliged to sit in gloom, with the aircraft windows blanked off so as to make the screen more visible. Many others simply wish to sleep in an attempt to counteract jet-lag. At least Tom had six days in which to gently slip into another frame. Arriving at JFK there is no pomp and circumstance. Customs clearance, even if you only have a visa waiver card, is without fuss and took me 20 minutes to complete. I avoided being cheeky to any customs officers.

TD

Yes, I really am in New York, and, released from the Custom-house, go direct to the Hoffman House; a grand hotel, run on the English and American system and everything is remarkably good.

Now I am hardly vain enough to think that this book will be read very much beyond my own circle of friends; but should any copies get further afield, I hope no readers will take offence to anything I have to say. I would ask them to remember that I am simply recording my impressions of what I saw; and if I saw things that didn't please me, I shall say so, just as I shall do about things that did please me.

Well, my first impressions about New York were that it was a wonderful place; but I had not been there long before I came to the conclusion that the streets were the worst I had ever seen, and I am still of this opinion. I suppose the reason is that it is such an awfully busy place, and everyone is so much on the rush striving to make money, they have not time to look after such matters as cleaning the streets or keeping them in good order. It is a busy place, a very busy place indeed; and really everybody seems wild on the one idea – make money. I asked an American, soon after I got there, what was the use of all this rush and bustle and excitement? What came of it? Was there anything attached to it? What did men do after they had made their pile? He simply replied, 'I guess they die.'

MG

Yes, New York is truly remarkable – a kind of electric atmosphere prevails which never lets up. I liked Simone de Beauvoir's quote in *America Day by Day*. 'There is something in the New York air that makes sleep useless.'

The Hoffman House Hotel no longer exists, but I was not

unimpressed by my abode. I must explain that prior to my 'excursion' I wrote to many hotel groups explaining my 'mission'. One of the major differences in hotels today from that of Tom's, is that we now live in the era of international hotel groups. I was lucky in that the Hilton Group kindly offered me concessionary rooms for much of my journey. By the time my trip would end these rooms felt like home. They worked.

I stayed at the New York Hilton & Towers, New York's largest with 2041 guest rooms and suites. I could not help but laugh at Tom's description of New York streets – even 100 years later they are in urgent need of repair. In all honesty however, I was much impressed by the lack of litter, but more importantly, a 'safer atmosphere' due, I was told, to the determination of the new mayor who has purged the city and increased the police presence on the streets. New York is still the place to chase money and this is now epitomised by Wall Street.

TD

Everybody knows the style in which New York is built – long streets running north and south called avenues, and then other streets running crossways from east to west. The square style seems strange to a European at first, and hardly takes his fancy; but afterwards, when the utility of it is seen, he alters his mind. It is certainly easier to find one's way about when told one's destination is, say, Fifth Avenue, Twenty-fourth Street, than it would be to a stranger here if told, say Duke Street, St. James's.

New Yorkers are very hospitable people, and I was treated right royally wherever I went, and was made an honorary member of most of the best clubs. These clubs are very elaborate affairs, and far more gorgeous than those we are accustomed to on our side.

The commercial buildings of New York are enormous, running from 12 to 16 storeys high; but, luckily, it is not necessary to tramp upstairs if you want the top floor, for the 'elevators' shoot you up to the top almost before you have time to take your seat.

My first cab drive was what they call an 'eye-opener' to me; for although I only went a short distance, the fare was a dollar. After that I gave up on cabs, and used the 'street-car.' Everyone uses the car, and I am not surprised at it, for the horrible streets make you think of 'the rocky road to Dublin'; and then the fare is very moderate, for five cents will take one anywhere. Cabs are very dear and very bad. The elevated railroad is by no means a bad way of getting about, and it is used very extensively.

I took a boat…that goes under Brooklyn Bridge, so one gets a very good view of this from all points; and it is not surprising that Americans are so proud of this picture of refined engineering skill, for it is really, as they say, a 'most elegant' structure. Then one gets almost a better view of the great Statue of Liberty than when arriving on a liner; and the statue is certainly worthy of all praise bestowed upon it, although in describing it the well-known modesty of the American comes to the fore.

MG

The streets are indeed 'easy', but since Tom's wanderings are deceptive in scale, I found myself walking for miles. Yes, New Yorkers are hospitable and although I missed out on the club scene, I enjoyed many hostelries. Tom's street cars no longer exist as such, being replaced by the notorious subway. I left the hotel and entered the subway on 7th Avenue, 53rd Street. Down below it was hot and stuffy even though it was mid-December. There was a strong smell of urine here and many of the homeless were sleeping on the hard bench seats, their belongings scattered around in black polythene bags. My train journey from mid-town to Wall Street would cost me about £1. Returning by yellow cab would set me back £8. Cabs are still dear.

I wanted to visit the USA's second-tallest building – The World Trade Center, at 110 floors and 1,377-ft high. The express elevator whisked me up to the top in just under a minute. Your ears pop at the change in air pressure. The view outside is breathtaking and the guide informed us that you could actually see the earth's curvature on the horizon. I also learned that a certain Phillip Petit on 7 August 1974 walked the tightrope between the building's twin towers and three years later a George Willig ascended the main building by using rubber suckers on his hands and feet.

Afterwards I headed down to the South Street Seaport, near Wall Street. From here I could savour a marvellous view of the Brooklyn Bridge. Feeling peckish I ventured into the North Star Pub. I was made most welcome and asked for a Dewar's Scotch whisky, to be told that they had none – but did have 'Dooers'.

Lunch was clams in a beer batter with potato skins washed down with a pint of Bass. I thought of Tom arriving nearby here 100 years ago and tried to imagine the hustle and bustle of the quayside then, standing in the shadow of the recently built Brooklyn Bridge.

I spoke with Roy the barman explaining my interest in the bridge. He explained that it was in a desperate state of disrepair. The toll money gained from the traffic passing over it does not go for repair work on the bridge, but subsidises the subway system. Today Seaport is very much a trendy place where Wall Street executives try to grab a few minutes of

tranquillity. Their constantly-ringing mobile phones began to irritate me so I headed back to mid-town. New York sparkled more than usual with Christmas only a week away.

I would be coming off Tom's trail for a few days to spend Christmas with my brother and his family in Richmond, Virginia. There I would witness my first 'ice storm'; beautiful in its crystal-glass sculpturing of landscapes, but deadly for motorists.

But before heading south for Christmas, the cities of Boston, Chicago and Washington beckoned.

CHAPTER 2

NORTH AMERICA: BOSTON, CHICAGO, WASHINGTON DC

BOSTON

TD

Now, it may not be generally known in this country, but it is well known in Boston, that there is one place in the world, and that is Boston. Everything here is extremely proper – in fact, almost ultra-English. There are heaps of people in this headquarters of 'cult' who would much rather be found dead on Boston Common than live for ever in a double-barrelled mansion in Michigan! In fact I have heard that when the first real Bostonian died and went aloft, St. Peter hesitated to let him through the gate; and upon the defunct one expostulating, and saying he came from Boston, St. Peter remarked that that was just the difficulty. 'However,' said he, 'come in; but *please don't be disappointed!*' I fancy there must be a bit of satire intended somewhere in that. It is certainly an important place, and the remarkable interest taken by natives in literature, science, and art is well known. This interest, too, is real in a way, for the place contains an enormous number of literary and kindred societies.

It is one of the old places, and was founded in 1630, so that naturally there are some old parts in the city, and these contrast strangely with the more modern districts. The city has been added to from time to time, and its area and population are steadily increasing; consequently the inhabitants get more and more important, in their own estimation, and think they are more than ever entitled to dub their city the 'Hub of the Universe.' Well, their doing so pleases them, and doesn't hurt anybody else; so what does it matter? Names don't hurt a bit.

A stranger might almost imagine that Boston was owned by some clothing syndicate, for the prominent advertisement all over the place is, 'Do you wear pants?' I suppose 'pants' is a more cultured word for 'trousers'. There really appear to be such a lot of people selling 'pants', it seems strange there should be anyone left to buy them. Some people think that Boston must have been founded by some patriotic Highlanders, and that, when the highly cultured era set in, the more advanced of the inhabitants began to look askance at the national costume of 'bonnie

Scotland'; therefore some enterprising Yankee immediately seized upon the opportunity to start a 'pant' business, and, prospering so much, rapidly brought around him a whole crowd of competitors.

MG

I departed Penn Station, New York on the 12.35 to Boston which left on schedule. The Amtrak carriage was very comfortable with lots of legroom and reclining seats. I felt pleased with my brief encounter with New York and I settled back to enjoy my six-hour journey along the North-eastern seaboard. However, the pinking mobile phones, which started to irritate me, meant that a pair of earplugs were the order of the day.

Urban scenes persisted for about an hour and then suddenly the last tower blocks disappeared and we were into the countryside. Stanford and Newhaven rolled past and occasionally I caught glimpses of the grey Atlantic Ocean. Sailing must be a pretty serious summer sport here as there were countless inlets crowded with berthed yachts. For their winter lay-up, they had been mummified in a kind of extra-wide cling film.

My hotel that evening was the Boston Back Bay and the room was lovely – it immediately made me regret travelling alone. Three walls of windows surrounded an enormous bed. The view was magnificent, some 20 floors up.

I awoke the next day to the sun pouring into my room. Feeling in need to get in touch with home I phoned my publisher, something Tom would have been unable to do. I was a little concerned that no 'story' seemed to be lurking here. He suggested I get out and about and visit some of Boston's bars and not try too hard to look for stories that weren't there. 'Don't worry, something is bound to happen sooner or later. Keep your eyes peeled,' he suggested. As he spoke wafts of smoke wisped past the windows of my eyrie. Putting down the phone I walked over to the window and gazed down on to the urban landscape below. Crowds of people with blankets over their shoulders were evacuating the adjacent Marriott Hotel. It was on fire!

It was to prove a very minor affair thankfully, but things were looking up on the story front. I took myself off to the Cheers Bar on 84 Beacon Street. It was a bitterly cold and windy walk from the Hilton, but it was dry and sunny. I chuckled at the albeit few 'pant' (trouser) shops en route and eventually arrived at what is probably one of the most famous bars on earth. But it's nothing like the bar we see in Cheers, which is pure studio set. I went down the entry-way stairs into a cramped, but cosy, howff. The bartender pulled me a pint of Guinness. Billy Burke and Chris Hawkes were the staff that day and had their own business cards to prove it. They were to prove a wealth of local knowledge. The cellar pub was very much like my local back home in Elgin: traditional dark wood, low ceiling, dimmed lights and a bar you can sit at *with* a brass rail to hold on to. The

speciality on the food front was New England Clam Chowder made with bacon, Maine potatoes, fresh clams and cream – it was delicious and reminded me of our Scottish Cullen Skink soup, but when I told Billy this, he was insistent that chowder was not soup! Oh dear...

Less well known but equally tasty was Boston Baked Beans; made with plenty of molasses, brown sugar, onions, seasoning and sliced hot dogs. Billy informed me that molasses used to be 'big' in Boston. Bigger than 'pants', I pondered. He went on to explain that this dark syrupy liquid was stored in the area during the early 20th century in enormous wooden vats, some capable of holding up to two million litres. During an unusually hot summer one of these enormous vats had been filled to the brim, allowing no room for expansion. The result was a catastrophic explosion which killed 21 people and destroyed six buildings. They say that in the summertime, even to this day, you can still detect the sweet smell of molasses in the basements of the older buildings, which had been flooded during the incident. I tried to imagine the mess, and wryly thought of the explosive qualities of molasses...and baked beans.

I explained to Billy that my next port of call was the 'windy city' of Chicago. He seemed a bit perturbed at me saying this and informed me that Boston was in fact more 'windy' than Chicago. 'It's all that hot air spouting from political debate down there,' he said. Baked beans came to mind again.

Feeling warmed up and well watered I headed to another bar, which was recommended by Billy; 'The Littlest Bar', just up the road. On the way I was intrigued and charmed by the gas street lighting which would have set the scene in Tom's day. The bar was as its name suggested: small, couthy and accommodating a maximum of perhaps ten customers. It was Irish, full and noisy but I did manage somehow to squeeze in. (Past politicians in Boston have been known to frequent this establishment but there was little room for 'hot air.')

The TV behind the bar was showing scenes of the bombing of Iraq by American and British aircraft; the other major news was the impending impeachment of President William Jefferson Clinton. What news might Tom have been exposed to in the Boston he visited? News of war would have arrived days or even weeks after the event, and I have to admit, as I viewed the scenes of destruction, I rather envied his position.

I found Boston an agreeable and safe place. There is a floodlit walking route around the city centre and as Tom rightly observed, culture and education clearly have played an important role here. But I had little more time to spare and I left the city with regret that I had not done it

justice. There is an atmosphere to Boston which requires more time than a stopover allows in which to fully appreciate it.

*   *   *

CHICAGO

TD

It is really almost difficult to know how to start upon this chapter, for Chicago is certainly a most wonderful place, and one can hardly realise that it is little more than twenty years since it was practically a heap of cinders. The terrible conflagration, which occurred in October 1871, will never be forgotten. Starting in a small barn on the south-western outskirts of the city, and not being attended to with the usual alacrity, the fire rapidly spread amongst the wooden buildings, and the wind blowing towards the north-east carried sparks and blazing fabric along with it, so that new fires were continually starting. It reached the river, and, though this is about one hundred feet wide, it proved no obstacle to the raging element, and to the horror and consternation of the crowds it was seen that the fire had crossed the river!

Widening as it went along, the fire, fed as it was by the wooden houses of which the place chiefly consisted, soon got beyond human control, and swept at its own sweet will in one vast wave of flame over acres and acres of ground, leaving behind it black ruin, desolation and death.

And now, what do we see? Not only a well-built city with handsome public buildings, lofty and substantial places of business, good streets, and indeed everything civilisation and science can suggest, but the most flourishing and rapidly increasing city in the States.

Tobacco-chewing is carried on strongly here – even more so, I imagined, than anywhere else, although the average American is never without his 'quid.'

When I first went out in Chicago I really thought that the ladies were indulging in the same habit, for almost every one I met had her little mouth working away most industriously at something or other; but luckily it turned out to be nothing more harmful than 'gum.' The retailing of 'chewing gum' is a very profitable affair in the States. This gum is pretty well guaranteed to cure 'the thousand natural ills that flesh is heir to', especially 'pepsin gum.' Having gone thoroughly into the merits and demerits of this gum-chewing business with the fair and sprightly stall-keeper of the article in the hotel hall, I one day yielded to her tempting and started a chew myself. I got on all very well for about a minute, and then the confounded stuff began to get into shape, and would stick about wherever there was a tooth to lay hold of. At last with a smothered blessing – which I need not repeat here – that gum was dismissed, and I registered a vow never to try the same game again.

I was pleased to see one thing, and that was, that although the ladies chew so much, they have not yet acquired, at least in public, that other habit of the male sex – expectorating! Spittoons are quite an essential piece of furniture, well, not alone in Chicago, but all over the States and they are to be seen in every room, store, hall – in fact, everywhere.

It doesn't matter what you want in Chicago, you can get it; and if the people have never heard of it or seen it before, they'll make it while you sit down and have a quiet 'chew.'

The buildings are very high in some parts, and some run up to as many as twenty storeys. Elevators are very much in evidence in these tall edifices, and there are two sorts – the ordinary and the express. The express is marked, 'This lift does not stop below the ninth floor'; and when you get in, and the thing is 'discharged', up it shoots – you fancy the moon at least is going to be your destination, especially if you get 'expressed' up to the eighteenth or nineteenth floor; but really, before you have got over the sensation of starting you have got to the stopping-place. The ordinary doesn't go beyond the eighth floor, and doesn't go quite so fast, but still there is not much difference.

MG

I arrived at the Hilton & Towers Chicago at around mid-day. The hotel was full to capacity with pre-Christmas shoppers obviously attracted by the hotel's central location and free bus service to the principal shopping malls. My first port of call was the historic and aptly named Chicago Water Tower. The tower, which stands at Michigan and Chicago Avenues, was erected in 1869 to house a 138-ft high standpipe, three feet in diameter. This standpipe served to equalise hydrostatic pressure in the mains system and minimise the pulsations of water flowing through the system. The tower was constructed of Juliet limestone blocks quarried in Illinois, a foresight which proved invaluable two years after its completion when, on the morning of 9 October 1871, flames engulfed Chicago and levelled nearly every building…except the Water Tower.

On the day following the fire, the tower served as a vital landmark for rescuers and citizens alike, hunting through the ruins for survivors and the remains of their homes. It has since become a monument to the efforts of Chicago's water works engineers and has remained a symbol of Chicago's indomitable 'I Will' spirit.

Across the road lies the gothic-style building of the Chicago Avenue pumping station. The automaton guides informed me that the pumping capacity of the 'station' is over 250 million gallons of water per day. Curiously, the inside reminded me of a brewery – spotlessly clean and

gleaming with brass and copper pipes, pumps and machinery. Nae spittoons here, or baccy chewers.

Within this building is Chicago Flat Sammies Restaurant which boasts that: '*Flat Sammies (Pat.Pending) is our revolutionary, old-fashioned way to make great sandwiches. Our bread is a blend of premium midwestern wheat, pure Lake Michigan Water, & proud Chicago Ethic.*' I could not resist the grilled pesto chicken served with four cheeses, Roma tomatoes and fresh basil. As I grazed contentedly on this marvellous creation, I could hear the incessant sound of the tourist hansom cabs above the automobile horns. There seemed to be little respite from the buzz of the city even for a short snack. Recollections of languid lunches consumed at a leisurely pace in the Craigellachie Hotel above the streaming waters of the Spey came to mind. But this was Chicago...

With my hunger satisfied I then went in search of America's tallest building; the Sears Tower. When I say tallest, this is debatable, because much of this claim lies in the length of the antennae on top of the building! But let's not get pedantic about the issue...it is a simply phenomenal structure of 110 storeys amounting to 1,454 feet in height. In less than 70 seconds an express elevator rockets you to the top and from the observatory you can view the beautiful city lakefront, the Lincoln Park Zoo, Soldier Field, Comiskey Park and four neighbouring states. On coming back down

to earth (again, in 70 seconds), I headed back to the hotel to partake of some liquid refreshment. I needed it.

TD

Any description of Chicago, however slight, without mention of its gigantic stock-yards would be no description at all; for I don't think I am wrong in saying that, occupying nearly 350 acres of land, they make the largest live-stock market in the universe. I thought I had seen a lot of remarkable sights in America one way or another; but when I went to have a look over these yards, and the slaughter and the packing-houses, I was fairly bewildered. Let me say, to start, that the places are simply enormous, and that a regular network of railway seems spread all around.

The first establishment I was taken to I entered the refrigerator warehouses. Not very sultry here, I will admit, but hundreds of carcasses were hanging around; and another department just here was simply for cutting up. Seemingly various joints of beef were flying all over the place, the different joints falling in front of a man; and they all seemed to know the man they had to go to, for each operator carves away at a similar joint all day. All they have to do is to clear the bone of meat. The man appears to give the joint three or four slashes with a big knife (just like I used to do with a sword, when in the Yeomanry, doing 'head-and-posts') to clear the bone; then the beef tumbles into one receiver to be trundled off to be tinned, or preserved, or made sausages of, or something like that, while the bone is thrown into another receiver, from whence some of it goes to be converted into knife-handles etc., but the majority to be boiled up for soup, and then ground down, mixed up with other things, and turned into a fertiliser.

The killing department is the one, though; and that, as well as the pig-killing place, quite staggered me. It seems very simple, however. There is an elevated platform by some loose-boxes, and upon this a 'man of good proportions', with an enormous 'quid' of tobacco visible in his upper lip, promenades up and down, manipulating a huge sledge-hammer the while. Two men are continually filling these loose-boxes with oxen (or steers, as they are called on the other side); and as soon as both animals arrive, one is greeted by the gentleman on the platform, who, swinging his huge sledge-hammer round, allows it to alight on the animals forehead; the other undergoes a similar welcome, and, both falling in a heap, the floor tilting up, they are shot through into the skinning department, where another gentleman receives them 'kindly like' (as Americans say) with another sledge-hammer, in case the first blow has not had the desired effect. A chain is then fixed to the hind leg, and in almost less time than it takes to write the steer is hanging up from a sort of suspended tramway or trolley arrangement and starts on his journey.

The first man skins the head and cuts it off, then passes the animal on to four men, who just jump on it and skin it with about the same ease and celerity with which a street ruffian whips off his coat when he wishes to engage in the 'noble art.' Then there are other cutting and slicing operations; but everything is done with such clockwork regularity that the time taken up between the entrance of the steer into the box and the final operation is comparatively little more than it has taken to write it.

From this it will be seen that, should the animal be only stunned by the sledge-hammers, the rapidity of the subsequent operations entirely prevents any return to consciousness. At the same time there is a story that a man once had six weeks in the infirmary suffering from a broken leg, caused by a kick from the hind leg of a steer soon after it had been decapitated, skinned, and disembowelled. I was introduced to a gentleman who confirmed this story; it seems hardly probable, but then it must not be forgotten that America is a wonderful country. Nothing whatever belonging to the animal is wasted; everything is utilised and turned into money. The horns go to Paris and other parts to be made into knife-handles, combs etc.; the bones, as I have already described, are first boiled, and after being ground down are mixed with the stomach and blood, compressed into cakes, and sold as a highly useful fertiliser. Not only a fertiliser, though; for a lot of this hard compressed mixture is made into buttons, and eventually finds itself displayed in this form upon the smart tailor-made costumes now in such favour with the fair sex.

Ah, ladies, do you ever think where your buttons come from? But, to show the value of this fertiliser, before its efficacy was discovered the parts composing it were thrown away – in fact, it was a matter of expense carting it off; but now, through this item alone, one firm nets $100,000 per annum, or about £20,000. At the slaughter-house I inspected, the daily average 'kill' is 3,000 head of cattle.

MG

Having imbibed, recovered, showered and changed I went off to meet another fellow Scot from Elgin, my doctor's younger son. He runs Sedgewick's Irish Bar on (unsurprisingly) North Sedgewick Street, a five-minute taxi ride from the hotel. This is a very large and busy bar; dominated by one gigantic TV screen and countless other monitors. Everyone in here wore baseball caps, Levi jeans and had only one thing on their minds...sport. Or more precisely, American football. This seemed to be the sole preoccupation of the revellers. I tried miserably to catch the atmosphere, but it was lost on me.

Regardless of this, I was made extremely welcome and despite my most strident efforts, was not allowed to buy a single drink. Tobacco smoking, not chewing, was much in evidence, but again no spittoons. I enquired tentatively about Tom's fascination over slaughterhouses and received some very strange looks. This must go on *somewhere*, beef burgers *must* come from places other than McDonalds or Burger King?! No-one, myself included, wanted to really explore this avenue any further. Americans enjoy their fast food but don't like to know how it ended up between their patties.

Despite my hangover, my flight to Washington the next day was memorable. The cheeky crew on this United Airlines flight cheered me up no end. Instead of the usual pre-flight reminders to stow hand luggage in the overhead bins and in front of the seats, the steward announced, 'If there's any loose luggage around when I pass, it will be chucked out!' Followed by, 'This is flight number UA 492 to Washington. If you are not travelling to Washington Dulles you had better start waving your arms and screaming, right now!' The entire plane erupted. I could not imagine this scene on a British Airways flight.

Mary Baker stole the show for me. This huge, happy clucking hen of a woman poured the cocktails at $4 a shot. A hair of the dog was required and she produced an unusual brand of vodka for my Bloody Mary. 'If you don't like it, I will replace it with something else,' she offered. I replied, with an almost finished tumbler, 'Yuck, that was horrible.' Her warm eyes twinkled at my mischief-making and she surreptitiously produced another miniature. The flight went well.

*   *   *

WASHINGTON

TD

I went by the 'Blue Line' to Washington, and had my first experience of dining on the American cars. It was not at all a bad experience either. To be sure, the crust of the claret got stirred up a bit; but what did that matter? We were travelling about fifty miles an hour, and one can't expect an 'Amphitryon' on board a train. There was no need to grumble at anything, and my decision was good.

The difference between New York and Washington is almost as great as between Whitechapel on a Saturday night and Kensington on a Sunday afternoon. It is no business place, and the ceaseless rush after money, money, money, of New York is entirely absent.

MG

I arrived in Washington on the 10th anniversary of the Pan Am flight 103 bombing over Lockerbie and my mood was melancholic as I strolled past the Lincoln Memorial. The sky was grey and icy gusts cut through my winter coat. I had at least secured a hotel for the evening, wrongly believing the Clinton impeachment would fill the city at the weekend. The Washington Hilton was almost deserted and that evening I rattled about in the bar. I gazed over to the entrance to the hotel where, some years ago, a lone assassin had attempted to kill President Reagan.

TD

The streets in Washington are all well asphalted and wood-paved; they can hardly be called streets, though, for they are wide avenues, with plenty of trees, and are more like Parisian boulevards. Beautiful is really the only word by which the capital of the States can be fitly described. A kind of shudder goes through one when the place where President Garfield was shot is pointed out, for the idea of such a good man being shot in such a beautiful place is very repugnant

The Capitol is a magnificent erection. This building covers about three and a half acres, and is a kind of central building with two wings. It is surmounted by a great white dome made of iron. The wings are white marble, and the main building is built of freestone. But most people are now familiar with the photographs of the place, which are about everywhere, so I need not describe it. Marble is predominant in the interior.

It is the headquarters of the country, and the Hall of Representatives in the south wing is an enormous room containing space for 300 members and 1,500 spectators. The mention and remembrance of No.1 vault in the treasury is tantalising to a degree. It is 89x51x12 feet, and contains 93,250,000 silver dollars or between 19 and 20 millions sterling! The White House, the home of the President, is here; and, much to the astonishment of the patriotic official who showed me over the place, I was able to tell him something about what it contained. He was expatiating proudly on the fact that everything, or nearly everything was American-made, when I mentioned that he must not forget there was something from Scotland in the cellar. At first he looked hurt: but when I gave him my card, and he saw who I was, his countenance relaxed, and the meaning smile which beamed over it proved that he was as well aware as I of what had travelled from Perth to Washington some few months previously. Well, much as I would have liked to stay in this delightful place, I was obliged to 'move on'.

MG

Two days to Christmas.

I awoke early at 7am. I wanted to see a lot this morning before catching the 15.05 from Union Station to Richmond, Virginia. My first point of interest was en route to the Capitol. I don't know quite what drew me to it, but I was taken by its simple and elegant beauty. It was the Vietnam Veterans' War Memorial.

I remember growing up at a time when the TV news was constantly filled with reports and images of this war. Nearly 60,000 names appear on these vast tapering walls of dark stone. I noticed a small child tracing a name on to paper while being watched by a parent. This place moved me deeply.

At the Capitol building I entered through the same doors Tom would have passed a century before; these were framed in bronze by a Munich sculptor. Here I was, sitting in the House of Representatives, the day after the impeachment vote. The sense of drama was electric. It reminded me of a Roman amphitheatre – an arena of vast power – and one of the most potent symbols of democratic government in the world.

Union Station was awash with travellers in festive mood. I enjoyed some Buffalo Wings and a Czech beer in the Island Bar of this gorgeous station. I would now come off the Dewar trail for a few days and head to Richmond for Christmas.

CHAPTER 3

NORTH AMERICA: MONTREAL TO SAN FRANCISCO

MG

Christmas passed and after a period of 'recuperation' I resumed the trail on the 27th December. I flew first to Montreal, then on to Toronto and Winnipeg, finally joining the VIA rail system to Vancouver. I then had to arrive in San Francisco for the 1st and 2nd of January, 1999. Tom also visited Ottowa and Quebec City which unfortunately I could not fit into my schedule.

I loved Montreal with its chic Parisian style; you can get 'real' French bread here and practically everyone speaks the language. The temperature was well below freezing and this, coupled with the many bistro-style restaurants on offer, curbed my adventurous spirit. At the time of writing, Quebec State was in a political quandary. The buzz on the streets was of independence and the recent referendum was as close as it gets. I could not help but compare the position with that of my native Scotland. We would have our first elections in May 1999 for a devolved Scottish Parliament, an exciting period in Scottish history but, I couldn't help but cringe at the enormous cost of it all. I may sound a trifle unpatriotic in saying this but my head, unlike my heart, remains unconvinced. However, it is essential that the Scottish voice is heard, not just in Westminster, but also in the European Union. This chapter is not about politics however, so I shall stop. Canada calls.

TD

Upon leaving Quebec for Montreal, I had my first experience of that marvellous achievement of railway engineering and skill, which is rightly numbered amongst the wonders of the world – the Canadian Pacific Railway. There are railways and there are railways; but, go where you will, there is not at present any railway which system, management, comfort in travelling, and downright general excellence comes within miles of the Canadian Pacific. It reaches right away across the vast Dominion of Canada, from the Atlantic to the Pacific, and passes through country which simply beggars description. The arrangements for dining, sleeping, etc. are just perfect; in fact, the whole thing is in reality a moving hotel of unrivalled excellence. Many very interesting parts are passed between Quebec and Montreal, and the names of several of the places recall the old days of the French settlements around here. Montreal is not only very picturesque, but is also imposing in appearance, especially when looked at from the river front, for then the full effect is got of the gently rising terraces of which the city is built, and the grand background to the whole of the wooded heights of Mount Royal – a mountain standing over 700 feet above the level of the river. The city is well built, and the streets are good. The population is a mixture of English and French; and, although the latter are in the majority, the trade is controlled by the former, as they are wealthier and far more energetic and industrious. In fact, the French have kept the place back very considerably. Still, Montreal is the commercial and financial centre of the Dominion. There is plenty of money in the place, and there is more continually being made. The cold about here is very intense in the winter, and the frost at times is so great that goods trains have been run across the St. Lawrence on the ice instead of across the ordinary bridge. They say the winter is very enjoyable, though, as there are plenty of means of keeping the circulation going – sleighing, tobogganing, skating and suchlike. Loyalty to the Queen and the Union Jack is very much marked here; but really throughout the whole of Canada a strong loyal feeling towards the Empire is most observable on every side. Possibly I may have noticed this the more after hearing the Old Country slanged so much in the States, for the lower-class American considers it the right thing to 'go for' everything British. I may say that this is not the case with the more reasoning and common-sense American, though; and I was pleased to find it so.

Well, when one gets on the great American Continent, whether it be the States, or whether it be in Canada, a spirit of restlessness and anxiety to keep moving arises, and there is no help for it. The very atmosphere seems to be laden with a 'go ahead' idea, and go ahead one must. I 'cavorted' round the place, here, there, and everywhere and eventually found myself on board the Canadian Pacific again bound for Toronto. This is a very fine place, and, as in the other Canadian cities, the streets are good. So far, nothing has come up - no, down – to the level of New York in the matter of streets. Yes, Toronto is a very fine place, and I should like to have stayed there longer, especially as I met some friends of my late relative, the Hon. Alexander Mackenzie, a late Premier of Canada – I believe a much respected man, and who, as the story goes, started there as a bricklayer; but the spirit of travel was upon me, and, as I could almost hear the mighty roar of Niagara there was no staying still, so off I went to view that greatest of Nature's wonders – the Falls of Niagara.

And when I arrived there – what a sight!

I will not attempt to be eulogistic upon the subject, for it is one that has puzzled the heads of far wiser folks than I can ever hope to be. To do ample justice in words to the awe-inspiring grandeur of such a scene is simply impossible. The river Niagara is only about 36 miles long, and flows from Lake Erie to Lake Ontario; but in its course it makes a descent of 326 feet! Some 22 miles or so of the river are above the Falls, and at the commencement of its course no-one would imagine that the quiet and peaceful-looking stretch of water would ever develop into the indescribable torrent it does further down. However, it gradually gains impetus, its velocity becomes greater and greater, it breaks into furious rapids, when, Goat Island dividing it, one part of the river rushes madly on to the American fall, while the other part is impelled with terrific force round the other side of the island, and, arrived at the brink of the awful precipice, the huge volume of water hurls itself over into the depths below with a thunderous roar that stays in one's ears for days, and which has been heard at a distance of fifty miles. The fall on the American side of the river is about 1,000 feet broad, and the descent is between 160 and 170 feet. The fall on the Canadian side is in the shape of a horseshoe, and the outline is about 2,600 feet, with a descent of some 160 feet. It is estimated that about 15,000,000 cubic feet of water sweeps over this huge precipice every minute. Below the falls, again, is another scene most awful in its grandeur. It is possible to take a walk underneath the Falls, but, I should hardly recommend this kind of stroll to persons suffering from nerves. You go down a lift for about 60 feet to get to the edge of the river below, and then take your stroll. I went. I 'wasn't a bit frightened', but somehow I began to wonder how many wicked things I had done in my life, and whether I had been guilty of a very egregious crime in my juvenile days when, in order to lessen a plague of rats, my parents had allowed me one penny for every tail I brought them, and I had sold them the same tails two or three times over. Funny that such thoughts will spring up at such peculiar times, but they do, and this was a very peculiar time. A slight slip of the foot here is quite sufficient to bring the whole of one's past life before one with a rush.

The deafening rush and roar was such, any one would hardly think it possible to hear oneself think; but you can, and I thought the place was one where any one would feel much more comfortable after saying a hymn than 'saying a swear.' I hope no one will think I was nervous, because I am only recording my impressions, and one of these I remember, was that I was not nervous. Familiarity, however, breeds a certain contempt in time, and the natives and residents have found that, becoming used to the surroundings, the 'fine feeling' at first produced will soon wear off, and enable them to work upon the feelings of others. And they do. I said natives, but I think thieves would be the more appropriate word, for the souvenirs of the place purchased by visitors before the terrestrial thoughts have quite returned, are charged just about five times the price for which they can be obtained elsewhere. Then again, wicked men are supposed to take portraits of visitors against the falls; but the visitors are participators in this fraud, for they are really taken in a studio, and then a background of the Falls put in. I saw the barrel in which some idiot – I forget his name – went through the rapids, and also the place where, through his foolhardiness, Captain Webb met his death. The latter place is certainly not the spot I should select for a morning dip; neither would I like to emulate the intrepid Blondin and cross the Falls in mid-air on a rope.

The enterprising American stops at nothing; and when I was there, tunnelling operations were being carried on (in fact, were approaching completion) under the village of Niagara Falls for the purpose of utilising the water power of the Falls for electric lighting and tramways. It is calculated that about 200,000 horse-power will be obtained, and that the cost will be only $5 per horse-power per annum. New York is only 450 miles from here, but the syndicate contend that the power will be quite sufficient to work a line as far as there. After being 'rooked,' like every other visitor to the marvellous Falls, and taking a final look at the wonderful place, I took the train again and moved on.

MG

I have been to Toronto many times before and it remains my favourite Canadian city. This time however, I was to meet up with a whiskey colleague – John Hanna, and tour the surrounding countryside. I desperately wanted to visit the nearby Niagara Falls. Toronto, incidentally, rates number three in *The Economist* 'Quality of Life Index', beaten only by Auckland and another Canadian favourite of mine – Vancouver. The 1999 index is derived from 42 factors as diverse as personal security and political stability.

From Toronto city the Falls are about a two-hour drive along the Niagara escarpment through fruit orchards and vineyards. Given that we were in wine country, we somehow managed to stop at many vineyards on the way; one in particular had a highly recommended restaurant and we were not disappointed. It was called 'On the Twenty' and was part of the Cave Springs Vineyards. Our starter was roasted St David's peppers filled with goat's cheese and basil followed by lamb shank braised in tomato and Gamay on a white bean ragout. This set us up for the day. What struck me, however, was their delicious dessert wines, called 'Icewine'. These Riesling grapes are kept on the vines after ripening, until the first frosts arrive. They are covered in sacking to protect them from scavenging birds, and once temperatures reach -10°c are pressed frozen to produce tiny amounts of nectar-like dessert wine renowned for its richness and concentration. The proof was naturally in the 'pudding'. They reminded me a little of French Sauternes and were similarly priced. Warmed by our meal and the wine tasting, the falls beckoned.

Like Tom, I found the effect breathtaking – the sheer enormity and natural power is awe-inspiring and, funnily enough, difficult to describe or capture in words. This really had to be seen and, above all, heard. You feel the tremors and hear the roar long before you see the cascading torrent. Tom describes the scene wonderfully and this wonder of nature has hardly changed at all since the dawn of humankind.

We did not linger for long, however, as the freezing mists chilled us to the bone. Already one third of my travel time had been expended, so the need to move on was very real. My next port of call would be even colder – I flew to Winnipeg to be welcomed by a temperature of -20°c and the cold speared me on the short walk between the terminal and taxi. I had never felt anything like it before, and was grateful to my thick and very old 'Crombie' coat. In any event, I knew that in a few days' time I would be entering much warmer climes.

The reason for visiting Winnipeg was to pick up the Canadian luxury train bound for Vancouver. Trains in this region, like the world over, have lost much of their vogue; airlines and highways have had a devastating effect on them. This VIA locomotive was more for tourists than the trains of Tom's day which carried settlers, miners and goods alike. To take this locomotive is, in itself, a journey back in time. You can discover how the West was won in true Canadian style as you retrace the historic western transcontinental route that, early this century, opened the West and created a bond of steel that redefined this nation.

The journey of 2,800 miles begins in Toronto, but would in Tom's time have started from the American eastern seaboard. Much of the modern-day line follows the original Canadian Pacific track but on nearing the Rockies it takes a more Northerly route. Construction began in 1871 and finished 14 years later, at 'Craigellachie BC' when both construction teams met up to drive in the last 'spike'; a bit like the French meeting the British in the Channel Tunnel.

The three-day rail journey took me past the lakes and forests of Ontario, the prairie plains, the Red River, then steadily rising terrain and through the stunning Rockies, before descending down to the Pacific. It ended at Main Street Station, Vancouver. Despite the blizzard conditions, it was the trip of a lifetime.

The 'Canadian' is not cheap, but it has great comfort, with its art-deco style and comfortable private rooms. The Park Car is wonderful with wraparound windows enclosing the Bullet Lounge. Above is the 360° scenic dome which provides awe-inspiring views. Nature here truly takes your breath away and at -28°c outside, that's hardly surprising. I think perhaps the fall would be the most beautiful time to make this trip, when the colours of the landscape can add so much to the experience. Vancouver lay at the end of the line and Tom described it wonderfully, before continuing on his way to San Francisco, just as I was to do.

The train arrived on time – I was pleased to step down and gasp at the chilling air. The train journey had been fantastic, but I was beginning to feel claustrophobic and although my travelling companions could not have been more courteous, I wanted to be alone; dine alone and smoke alone!

*   *   *

Vancouver
and San Francisco

TD

Getting towards a place called Langevin, a little excitement springs up, for it is here that one gets a first sight of that wonderful range of mountains, the Rockies. It is just the higher peaks of them that can be seen, provided the day be clear, and from here prairies, ranches and seas of waving grass begin to disappear and a great change comes over the face of the earth. While travelling on the American route, one might well have put in his diary, 'This was a wheat day', 'All corn again today' etc.; but here things are different, and the acres and acres of prairie give place to the wild and magnificent grandeur of the Rockies. During the whole trip on this train we had been gradually ascending above the level of the sea, till, at a place called the gap, an altitude of 4,200 feet was reached, as against the 700 feet at Winnipeg.

But the gap! This is the entrance to the Rockies, and is a fine foretaste of the scenery that is to come. Just before reaching this place, the Kananaskis river is crossed by a high iron bridge, and the sensation going over is peculiar in the extreme, to say the least of it; especially when, as I experienced it, the sun is just rising and shedding a warm, ruddy glow all around. High above the river the train rolls along, and as one is looking at the rapid current below and listening to the roar of the great Kananaskis Falls – capped with snow and ice, and tinted with the rays of the rising sun, the majestic Rocky Mountains seem to come abruptly forward, and almost before one is aware of the change the train goes round a curve and is between two vertical walls of rock, the height of which seems almost immeasurable; in fact, the Rockies have been entered. From here to Vancouver is one vast and imposing panorama of magnificent scenery. But how to describe this rugged, weird and awe-inspiring view is beyond me. There is too much to describe in a few lines, or even a few pages; it is simply a series of fascinating and beautiful pictures of Nature in all her wild grandeur. Here, ranges of huge mountains of dizzy height, forced, as it were, from the depths of the earth below, and showing their strata as plainly and distinctly as before any disturbance, and looking as though they would every moment press forward and demolish the contrivance which the ingenuity of man has devised by which to enter their sacred presence; now through the gorge, a vast space opens up to view, almost barbaric in its splendour, with here and there the charred remains of trees and brushwood destroyed by fire caused by the sparks from locomotives; now high up, running along the side of a mass of rock, while below are rivers and rushing mountain torrents – no, no, I will not attempt to describe it; I will simply say the whole sight held me spellbound.

Just before getting into Vancouver, at a station – for some reason or another, goodness only knows what – I shouted to the engine-driver of the train in Gaelic, and to my astonishment, and also that of the shooting party I was with, he replied in the same terms; not only replied, but rattled out such a lot

– he was a Scotchman – and was so pleased to hear the language again, he almost forgot all his duties connected with the train. Vancouver is a very nice place, and very pleasantly situated at the mouth of the Fraser River, on a large bay in which a quantity of shipping is always lying, including one or other of the magnificent steamships recently built by the Canadian Pacific Railway Company to connect Vancouver with Japan. The harbour here is classed amongst the finest in the world, and there can be no possible doubt but that the city has a very good future in store. Times were good, and the place is prospering wonderfully; it only wants time to develop into perhaps the most important city in British North America. A peculiar thing is that it is the only place which has not been thoroughly boomed and worked up, as it were, artificially. It has grown rapidly, but genuinely; and no-one can quite realise that in 1885 the site was a dense forest. Yet such is the case, and it was May 1886 when wooden houses first began to spring up, and they grew almost like mushrooms till the end of June, when there was a bit of a stoppage, for a big fire burnt down every house in the place, with one solitary exception. Almost before the ground got cool the inhabitants were at work building again; but this time they tried stone, bricks and mortar, and laid the place out with a bit of method. The streets are good, and well lighted both by gas and electricity; while some of the buildings, both public and private, would do credit to any city that could be mentioned. It is a wonderfully English place, and there are only a very few Americans and Canadians included in the 20,000 inhabitants which it now boasts of – not nearly so many as one would expect to find in a rising place occupying such a commanding position. There is plenty of room for another 20,000 people, or even treble that number; in fact, the cry all over the place is, 'Labour with Capital.' The two must go together; and for any one with a small capital, and able to work, Vancouver would be by no means an undesirable place. This must not be confounded with Vancouver Island, of which Victoria is the capital, for that is some distance away. Small-pox was on the rampage on this island when I was at Vancouver (in fact, the 'yellow flag' was out at various houses in Vancouver); so I didn't ferry across to it, but satisfied myself with reading and hearing about it and looking at photographs.

MG

Unfortunately I would have little time in Vancouver, as my next flight to San Francisco was only six hours away – but lunch beckoned! I chose the Seasons Restaurant in the beautiful Queen Elizabeth Park. It is located at Vancouver's highest point and offers matchless views of the city's stunning skyline with the Coast Mountains in the background. For lunch I chose Surf & Turf which consisted of half a Pacific lobster, and a pink fillet of pan-seared beef. The sauce was puréed scallops and crab in cream and dill, and a crispy and colourful side salad finished this dish off. I washed this down with a light and refreshing rosé from Chateau Peyrassol in Provence.

Chinese restaurants are also prevalent here and the city has always acted as a gateway to the Far East with many Cantonese and Japanese living here. Many Hong Kong Chinese came here when the former British colony changed hands recently. This is hardly surprising as Vancouver sits at number one in *The Economist* magazine's 'Quality of Life Index' mentioned earlier.

I have visited Vancouver before, in the late spring, and it is a truly beautiful city. I particularly liked the integration of housing and apartments in the city centre, in stark contrast to most modern cities, where nobody seems to live in the centre. The sea surrounds the city, so you are never far away from nature. But nature today was at its most harsh and I was looking forward to the Californian sunshine and meeting up with some whisky colleagues of old.

TD

Now I get on board the train again, and make a real start for 'Frisco, the Golden City, stopping on the way at Mount Shasta to sample the water of the Shasta natural mineral spring, which is really very good indeed, and the sight of the water coming jumping up is very strange. The entrance to 'Frisco by this railway is not calculated to make one go into ecstasies over the place, for bogland and prairie have to be passed through; but this is not much, and once inside the Golden City all the objectionable and disappointing features connected with the entrance are forgotten. California is a wonderful fruit-growing country, and one farmer's story was that if any one planted his, say, 160 acres with fruit, with ordinary luck, after the third year, he should be making $5,000 a year net profit. There is a sort of blackberry-bush that grows to an immense size if properly cultivated. I didn't see it, but I was told that it was nothing for one of these *bushes* to cover one or two hundred yards of ground; in fact, if a man had room enough to grow a couple of them he could make a good living! Wonderful place, America! Everything so large about it! At least, not exactly *everything*; minute, and at the same time objectionable, things might be mentioned.

Well we're in the wonderful city of 'Frisco, and the Palace Hotel, where I stayed, is always popularly supposed to be the largest in the world; the manager says he isn't quite sure how many people he can accommodate, but he thinks he can put up almost 1,000 people! The Presidential election excitement wasn't quite over during my visit; and, I presume in order to stimulate the voters, a band of musicians – well that's what they called themselves – dressed as volunteers, discoursed a terrible row every evening in the courtyard of the hotel. It would really be a libel on a noble art to call the noise music, for each man seemed to be imbued with the idea that all he had to do was to blow down his instrument as hard and energetically as he possibly could, while diligently chewing his 'quid' at the same time. Those abominable nuisances about the streets of London, the German bands or hurdy-gurdies, are refinement compared with that conglomeration of hideous noises.

The streets in 'Frisco are very good, and the cable-car system is just A1. When the cable-car system was first introduced, it was altogether too much for John Chinaman; his celestial mind couldn't grasp the idea at all, and he looked upon it as something almost supernatural. 'No pullee, no pushee, go like helle,' John would say, and then jump over the lines. Nothing would induce him to *walk* across. He is getting to understand it now, though. Theatres, public-houses or 'saloons,' and churches abound all over the city, and all are well patronised. The Chinese are very numerous, and their quarter of the city, called Chinatown, is well worth a visit; but before taking a walk round, it is just as well for the visitor to prepare his nerves, and make up his mind not to be too squeamish, for during the whole tour he will be surrounded by dirt, stench, and immorality. I don't think I will go into details. There are a lot of French here, and the Irish muster are very strongly too in different parts, but perhaps more especially at Golden Gate Park, and they are all 'patriots'. While touring round there one day, I heard a story of a green parrot whistling 'Boyne Water,' much to the annoyance of Paddy. 'Och, ye divil,' said Pat, 'shure, its only your colour that saves ye! If ye were a canary, begorra, I'd wring your neck!' Poor Polly!

A long time can be very profitably spent in 'Frisco, for there is plenty to see, and the inhabitants are without a doubt 'all sorts and conditions of men.' One day I was very much amused. I had just been to a Republican meeting, the principal part of the speeches at which seemed to be 'Fellow-citizens'; and outside the hall some man was suddenly inspired, and, jumping on a barrow, commenced to harangue the crowd on the evils of intemperance. He hadn't got far when he was ignominiously pitched from his barrow, and the little attentions he received from his erstwhile hearers were such that the police had to interfere and protect him. Just before leaving 'Frisco, when I was buying a Kodak, another customer was doing the same, but keeping up such a lively chatter all the time that I was obliged to begin as well. On mentioning that I was leaving for Honolulu by the *Alameda*, he said, 'I'm pleased to meet you, Mr Dour' – (he couldn't fix Dewar) – 'for I guess that's who it is. Shake hands! I'm going on the same trip. What's your stateroom?' To our astonishment we found we were to share the same stateroom. A friend had given him an introduction to me; but, making a bold shot for it, he had anticipated events, and not waited till he got on board. He may possibly have the temerity to read through these pages, otherwise I should say that a nicer American, a more genuine man, or a livelier or jollier travelling companion I never met. But there are times when it is not advisable to say all one thinks, so I will pass over the gentleman's good qualities in silence; but as he kept me company for some months, he will have to be mentioned more than once again.

MG

I arrived in a warm and sunny San Francisco on the 2nd of January. Once again, the Hilton hotel was where I was to stay and it was awash with revellers. Near to the hotel I noticed a statue of Robert Louis Stevenson who, while searching for a friendly climate to aid his ailing health, lived in San Francisco for several years before moving on to Samoa. He died there and is remembered with great affection by the Samoans.

The trolley cars are great fun to ride on and, given the slope of the city streets, make a welcome respite. I headed to Fisherman's Wharf which, although crammed with tourists, sold beautifully fresh crab and lobster meat. (Incidentally, the Hilton Hotel contributes to the upkeep of the cable car system in the city.)

From the wharf, I took a short ferry ride to the sinister island of Alcatraz. In Tom's day, the island would have served as a defensive point guarding the entrance to San Francisco Bay. Although a fort and lighthouse did exist on the island at that time, it was not until after the Depression of the 1920s that the newly created Department of Justice became interested in the island as a high-profile, maximum security facility. In 1934 Alcatraz opened as a Federal Penitentiary.

Over 1,545 men did 'time' on Alcatraz and many were notorious – these included Al 'Scarface' Capone, 'Doc' Barker, Alvin 'Creepy' Karpis, George 'Machine Gun' Kelly, Floyd Hamilton and Robert Stroud, the 'Bird Man of Alcatraz'. Most of the other prisoners were men who were very difficult to confine elsewhere. Of the attempted escapes, the best known occurred in June 1962, when Frank Morris and brothers John and Clarence Anglin slipped unseen into the water. They used tied-up raincoats as flotation devices and were bound for San Francisco. Their bodies were never found.

As part of its security, the Bureau of Prisoners deliberately restricted visitors to the rock. This isolation helped to fuel stories of the inmates' miserable living conditions but, in fact, the prison was clean and the food was good. Increasing maintenance and operating costs led US Attorney General Robert Kennedy to close Alcatraz in 1963. The prisoners were dispersed to other correction facilities leaving Alcatraz in custodial care.

Today the island serves mainly as a tourist attraction. The tiny cells

are still there – with beds and cleaning utensils left intact. I immediately started to feel claustrophobic when entering them – heaviness bore down on me. We were told that, under certain weather conditions, the inmates would have heard the melodic cheer of the New Year's Ball across the water and the clink of glasses being raised. I was glad to be 'released' into the warming sun and felt relieved to get back to the city.

The following day, I met the whisky writer Gordon Christopherson and he kindly offered to drive me around the area. We drove to the gorgeous towns of Santa Cruz and Los Gatos. Santa Cruz was bathed in sunshine this early January day and many people were surfing offshore. Los Gatos sports California's most famous whisky bar – CB Hannigans which is managed by the legendary connoisseur Tom Ovens. His knowledge and enthusiasm for malt whisky is renowned and he made us most welcome. We enjoyed ribs in smokey barbecue sauce; enough to feed an army. Commenting to Tom on the generous helpings, he proceeded to explain the Celtic nature of the pub. St Patrick's Day celebrations are taken very seriously indeed, and the following list was the 'consumption' for that day last year!

ST PATRICK'S DAY, LOS GATOS CALIFORNIA
150 lbs. roasted pig
250 lbs. of pork roast
400 lbs. corned beef
300 lbs. of BBQ chicken

660 lbs. of ribs
100 lbs. of hot links
120 lbs. of Italian sausage
250 lbs. potato salad
20 whole turkeys
10 pans of shepherd's pie
3,800 oysters
120 lbs. mussels
77 kegs of beer
196 bottles of various liquors
62 gallons of Margaritas

Before leaving to return to San Francisco, we visited Santa Cruz where again many were out surfing, albeit in wetsuits. The sun was out, however, and the chill of the recent days seemed to be lifting.

TD

We left in the evening just before sunset, and dropped gently down the waterway which connects San Francisco Bay with the Pacific, the rays of the setting sun lending a glowing colour to the magnificent scenery we were leaving behind; but as the steamer glided on, and eventually steamed into the great Pacific Ocean, a more than beautiful sight burst upon us. Far away ahead were sparkling, dancing, blue rippling waves beneath which the monarch of the day was just dipping; while astern was the coast of that gigantic country across which I had travelled, the huge rocks on each side of the entrance to the bay we had left looking indeed the 'Golden Gates' they were called, for they were bathed in the glorious rays of that golden sun which was fast disappearing below the horizon. I'm a bit of an artist in a way, and must confess I was fairly carried away by this sight.

CHAPTER 4

SOUTH PACIFIC: HAWAII, FIJI, NEW ZEALAND

HONOLULU

MG

My flight the following day was delayed by two hours due to the horrendous weather conditions in Detroit and Chicago; the latter suffering 20 inches of snow in 12 hours. This had a knock-on effect at San Francisco Airport. But I was undisturbed as I had a good book with me and, besides, I was going to somewhere really exquisite. I pondered on the stark and varied weather conditions in this part of the world.

TD

Well, on the seventh day from 'Frisco we landed at Honolulu, and I had my first sight of real Pacific, tropical scenery. Although I was well acquainted with that to be found in Africa, Madeira, etc I had only seen the Pacific in imitations at various places both in England and America, in hot houses, gardens, theatres, etc; but now here was the real thing, and I almost felt that I must take up my abode amongst it forever.

The Hawaiian Islands are called the Paradise of the Pacific, and no better term could be applied to them. Palm-trees, cocoa-nut trees, bananas, oranges, flowers, ferns, – in fact, every conceivable kind of tropical vegetation, and all in profusion – a perfect climate, swept by ocean breezes, – what can one wish for more? It is fairyland in reality.

Honolulu, the capital of the group of islands, is a well-built and good business place. Like 'Frisco, it has a big Chinese and Japanese population, and Chinese labour is pretty general in the coffee, sugar and rice industries.

The mosquitoes here were remarkably chummy – in fact, quite embarrassingly so; and they bit me within about an inch of my life. There are twelve islands in the group, but four of them are barren; and a tour in a steamer round the lot will soon show anyone how it is that, as well as Paradise, etc, the 'Inferno of the World' is also so justly applicable; for here is found, if not the largest, the most remarkable volcano in the world. I cannot really say all I want to about these islands here, for it would make a book of itself, and I almost think I shall some day write one specially devoted to their wonders and their beauties. One island which no-one can visit without feelings of the greatest sorrow is that of Molokai; the home of the lepers, of whom there are some 1,100 or 1,200. Apart, however, from the sorrow arising from such a painful sight – although the lepers themselves seem happy and contented – one cannot help feelings of the highest admiration arising for those two really good, sincere and earnest men, Father Damien and Pastor Hanaloa, who lived and died in their work amongst the poor victims of this frightful disease, and whose bodies lie buried on the spot of their noble devotion and self-sacrifice.

MG

Arriving on this fabulous group of islands, I was immediately taken by the friendliness of the people. 'Aloha' was the standard greeting here – and tourist PR was of a high order. Many countries, including my native Scotland, could learn from this attitude to visitors! This part of the trip would be a five-day vacation – I desperately needed to rest up for a bit after some pretty extensive and exhausting travel.

The Hilton Hawaiian Village was bliss. I have experienced nothing quite like this: palm trees, exotic flowers, colourful parrots and flamingos and pools of radiant tropical fish. My room was in the Rainbow Tower overlooking Waikiki Beach. This must be as close to paradise as it gets – and not a whine of mosquito to be heard anywhere. The whole resort is manicured, not a cigarette butt or sand fly could be found on the beach – it was raked and sieved daily.

But I was saddened a little on entering my room – it overlooked the lapping, gentle ocean, a soft breeze rustled the nearby palms, a giant bed lay turned back with orchid petals on the massive billowy pillows. I was on my own. Oh, well.

Tourism is the business in Hawaii and over six million people visit annually. Fruit was exported from here in a big way until recently and in its heyday the Dole 'Pineapple' Company employed 1,300 people. Today that has shrunk to about 45. Mechanisation and foreign competition, particularly in south-east Asia has had serious repercussions for local employment. This, however, has been mitigated by the huge rise in tourism. Being a canny Scot, I did find the island expensive; particularly for food and drink but my brother, who had visited the island a few years previously, advised me of the 'World Food Market' which I enjoyed enormously. For $5 you could buy, from the numerous stalls, a full Chinese-style meal of sweet and sour pork and chicken with fried rice. On the drink side I found many ABC stores quite reasonable for beer, gin and whisky.

My last day in Hawaii was to prove very moving. I have avoided politics in this book, and the folly of man, but I could not help being stirred at my visit to Pearl Harbour and the USS *Arizona* Memorial. You take a small launch on a short journey to the 184-ft long memorial structure spanning the mid-portion of the sunken battleship. You can look down on

the rusting hulk which rests about two metres below the surface. Oil still seeps out, creating shimmering rainbows on the surface of the water around the wreck. The USS *Arizona* is the final resting place for many of the ship's 1,177 crewmen who lost their lives on the 7 December 1941. The memorial grew out of a wartime desire to establish some sort of memorial at Pearl Harbour to honour those who died in the attack.

According to its architect, Alfred Preis, the design of the Memorial, '...*wherein the structure sags in the centre but stands strong and vigorous at the ends, expresses initial defeat and ultimate victory. The overall effect is one of serenity. Overtones of sadness have been omitted to permit the individual to contemplate his own personal responses – his innermost feelings.*'

*   *   *

FIJI

My next flight was Pacific Airways to Fiji – Tom chose nearby Samoa. The flight took me across the 180th meridian adding a day to my journey. Arriving at Nadi Airport, I was immediately taken by the lushness and greenery of the surroundings. I disembarked and was hit by a wall of steamy tropical heat and I gasped in the sauna-like atmosphere. This island deep in the South Pacific is now a republic and is desperately trying to encourage tourists. You could not find a more idyllic setting with white coral beaches, dancing palms and turquoise-blue lagoons. It was very quiet and I imagined meeting Robinson Crusoe here. I was impressed by the politeness of the locals, Fijian and Indian alike. My hotel, family-run, was cheerful and fortunately had air conditioning in the bedrooms.

The prices were a change from Hawaii as well. A haircut here cost me about £1 in a stifling Indian barber shop. The cut-throat razor which he brandished caused me a little anguish, but his skills were well honed and the back of my neck was smoother than I could remember. He dusted me off

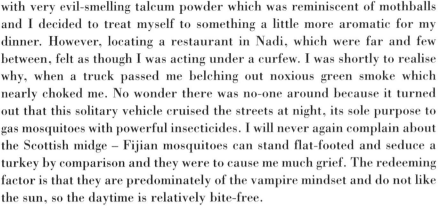

with very evil-smelling talcum powder which was reminiscent of mothballs and I decided to treat myself to something a little more aromatic for my dinner. However, locating a restaurant in Nadi, which were far and few between, felt as though I was acting under a curfew. I was shortly to realise why, when a truck passed me belching out noxious green smoke which nearly choked me. No wonder there was no-one around because it turned out that this solitary vehicle cruised the streets at night, its sole purpose to gas mosquitoes with powerful insecticides. I will never again complain about the Scottish midge – Fijian mosquitoes can stand flat-footed and seduce a turkey by comparison and they were to cause me much grief. The redeeming factor is that they are predominately of the vampire mindset and do not like the sun, so the daytime is relatively bite-free.

I was now well into a course of malaria tablets and having been subjected to a myriad of inoculations before starting my trip, I felt little concern. I was travelling at a time when some of the world's worst diseases have been eradicated; in Tom Dewar's day, and earlier, when Robert Louis Stevenson made his home in these parts, a host of diseases including smallpox, typhoid, malaria, cholera and yellow fever were prevalent. We tend to take for granted the fact that modern medicine is one of the wonders of the world.

TD

The drink of Samoa is kava, and there are two ways of making this – one the common or garden, and the other the royal method. My American friend and I went one day to see it made. The 'distillery' was a very large hut in the woods, and the working staff consisted of about five-and-twenty natives; but an admiring crowd had followed us to the place, so that there was quite an audience. The operation consists of grinding the root of the kava between stones, then putting it into a bowl and making it into a pulp, then straining it off. Great excitement was caused when I tried my hand at making it, and this increased tremendously as I proceeded; all the 'staff', as well as the audience, chattered and laughed so much and got so interested, it was quite amusing. One who spoke a little English said the cause of the excitement was that they all declared I made it as though I had always been in the business.

We tasted it – oh yes! we tasted it; and then, to show the generosity of the white man, we distributed the remainder amongst the crowd. They liked it; we were very glad they did. Reader, would you like to taste this native drink? If so, boil a cabbage, when it gets cold squeeze all the moisture out of it that you can, flavour with soft-soap, and drink it – you then get a very fair idea of what kava is like. But the royal method of making it is different, and this is only adopted by persons of high degree, and when they wish to pay more than ordinary honour to some distinguished personage. It is made by very young girls of from twelve to twenty years of age, having very good teeth; and the operation is very simple, for these girls simply chew the root and spit it into a bowl, instead of crushing it between stones! Several individuals, including my friend King Malietoa, were most anxious to extend this high honour to us; but we explained that we were very modest in nature, and, although we might be princes in our own country, we were travelling strictly *incognito*, and that, while we appreciated the proffered honour at its very highest, we begged to be allowed to decline it. The guide who took us all over the island to see the different sights was about the most perfectly modelled young fellow I have ever seen; and although he was but fourteen years old, he stood just over six feet high. He gave me three sittings in my Kodak, and this honour nearly made him another inch higher. The natives are very fond of tattooing themselves, and do it principally from the waist to the knees. They have evidently got an idea that this is quite sufficient covering to meet the demands of civilisation; for, although they are compelled by the authorities to have a covering over their loins, this is very slight, and they undoubtedly strongly object to it, for a week seldom passes but one or two are fined or sent to gaol for a bit for promenading *à la* Adam! The Samoese ladies adopt a kind of Mother Hubbard costume, which is by no means unbecoming; but I never cared to get too close to any of them, because of the amount of cocoa-nut oil about, which they considered necessary to enhance their beauty. Even my susceptible American friend 'guessed they would look more kissable to a Christian if they'd hold on a bit with the oil.

MG

At this point in my trip, I started to miss home. Pitiful I thought, considering the time that my predecessor had voyaged abroad. I tried to rationalise this feeling: in a way, I was rootless and simply globe-trotting, not spending any time really in any one place, or getting to know anyone to any degree, and no-one me. My melancholy was hard to dispel and I felt that I was passing through places for the sake of passing through them. In effect I was taking unconsciously RLS's advice in *Travels with a Donkey*. 'For my part, I travel not to go anywhere, but to go. I travel for travel's sake.' It's all very well trundling along in the Cevennes with a donkey for company, but I wonder how he would have felt in my shoes.

My gloomy mood was shortly to be alleviated on departing Nadi Airport to Auckland. When I first started travelling abroad on holiday or on business, I often was guilty of mistaking a stranger with a likeness to someone I knew back home. After several embarrassing taps on the shoulder I gave this habit up! At Nadi, however, a couple stood out from the rest. I was sure the man was a well-known businessman from my home town by the name of Charles Smith and I detected my own local dialect when I overheard him in conversation with his wife. The Bank of Scotland hold-all which he carried over his shoulder convinced me of his authenticity. For once I was right and we shared a very pleasant flight to New Zealand. It lifted my spirits no end to meet two fellow Scots in this very remote part of the world.

TD

There is nothing like variety to keep the mind well occupied and prevent one from getting dull; and here was another change.

The poetic and romantic Samoa, with its hundred and one attractions, had to be left; for although I would have gladly have followed the example of Robert Louis Stevenson and made the islands my home, to fulfil my mission I had other climates to sample. So with a good-bye sad and sorrowful, I once more packed up my nail-brush, sponge, slippers, and other *impedimenta*, and went on board a boat bound for New Zealand.

The different winds about kept the air delightfully cool; and now and then, when a current would take charge of the boat, we went along at a much increased speed. One day we ran for over forty miles with a current; and then in the morning we had about four hours' very nasty rolling about, caused, as I was told, from going with a current that ran between two mountains under the sea. It would be better if those mountains were taken away; the motion of the vessel is not pleasant when in their neighbourhood. Then we crossed the meridian, and had to skip a day in the almanac, so as to make matters right on the other side, and not be a day behind. They manage all these things very well at sea; there is no arguing about it – they just do it, and there you are. The sailors don't get docked or credited a day's pay, so they don't mind a bit.

MG

Before leaving Fiji I must take up Tom's point on passing the meridian or International Date Line. The new millennium will be a PR dream for the South Pacific island nations, as this is the area where each new day starts and ends and where visitors will be first to bring in the year 2000. As early as 1996 the South Pacific Millennium Consortium was launched in a bid to pool limited resources. However this collective effort soon fell apart as each island tried to steal the show. The heated debate centres on the location of the individual islands in relation to the International Date Line.

The position of the 180° meridian 12 hours ahead of Greenwich Mean Time was agreed in 1884 because it cuts through the Pacific Ocean rather than a landmass. However, a quirk appears as the Meridian is routed around areas like Samoa and Fiji: planes flying to the west of the Meridian are a day ahead of those flying to the east. Fiji seems to be the only country where the 180° meridian lies across land – on Taveuni and Rabi islands and at Vola Point and Vanua Levu. A globe at Nadi Airport rotates hourly in the countdown to the start of festivities.

Fiji's claim to being the place where the world's biggest party will begin has however been refuted by Tonga who are staking that claim for themselves. But it is a spurious claim considering that the islands lie 160 miles west of the date line! In any case, Caroline Island can claim to be ahead of Tonga by an easy 80 minutes, but its problem is that it is uninhabited. I don't fancy taking in the millennium on my tod. Caroline has actually been renamed 'Millennium Island'.

Lastly, according to the Royal Geographical Society, the South Pacific Islands' claims and counter-claims are irrelevant to their calculations. It will be on Mount Hepeha on Pitt Island in the Chatham Islands, 500 miles east of New Zealand at 1559 hours GMT on 31st December that the millennium's first dawn rays will appear.

As it happens, I shall probably be in my local pub at that time with good company and fine ale, and do not much care who will be first to see the New Year in.

*   *   *

AUCKLAND

TD

New Zealand is sighted, and before very long our anchor is dropped in Auckland harbour, and we are once more on dry land. I say 'dry land,' because I believe that is the proper phrase; but in reality the land was anything but dry – in fact, it was very wet, for it was raining very hard, and had been for some time. We were told that Auckland had more rain than any other town in Australasia; and we could almost believe it, for it was wet during by far the greater part of our stay there. And when I say wet I mean it, for the rain seems to be different from English rain. Its more like heavy Scotch mist, and seems to come from everywhere – not in drops, as ours does; and its pretty continual. However we did see what the fine weather was like, and our first experience of this was grand. The air was quite fresh and balmy, and we could quite understand the almost perfect climate of the islands which is so favourable to agricultural pursuits.

MG

I arrived in sunny Auckland in mid-January, 1999. For this visit I would be staying with a good friend by the name of Maggie Barretta. She previously hailed from Forres in north-east Scotland and is a definitive Scotswoman. Before arriving I had faxed her Tom's notes on his journey through New Zealand in the 1890's. Maggie studied these and then acted as a brilliant guide and I enormously enjoyed our wanderings around the North Island. Car hire was inexpensive and made very easy by driving on the left-hand side as in the UK. The climate was also perfect: warm summer sunshine with a gentle breeze and lush countryside.

TD

Auckland is a funny place, and a typically Scotch town. After the carefully and squarely arranged towns and cities of the States it looked a little 'straggly', but at the same time it certainly looked 'homely'. The 'fire-bell' arrangement is peculiar; these bells are all over the place, and, when a fire occurs, first one bell goes, then the other, and the engine turns out. The inhabitants also are very homely, although they look a bit rough.

Ah, if we could only get oysters in London at the same price as in Auckland! The best are 3d. per dozen, and by the sack even less than that! They lie in thousands on the north shore, and the only expense is gathering them. In hotels 6d. per dozen is charged; but even at that advanced figure one's lordly feelings arise, and oysters and stout are indulged in without giving even one thought to the expense. How different from the Whitstable native London, which is really no better! I was exceedingly lucky one day. My friend and I bought some oysters, and were having a jolly *al fresco* banquet; at the finish one oyster was left. Politeness forbade either of us taking it, so we 'matched' for it. We call it tossing, or, as I believe it is vulgarly called, 'Tommy Dodd,' but my Yankee friend would have it the proper term was 'matching.'

Well, I won, and the oyster was opened, and I found I was the possessor of two pearls as well, for these were in one shell. One was as big as a small pea, and, mounted for a scarf pin, looked remarkably well. The other one, inferior in every way, I handed to my friend as a consolation prize for losing.

MG

I enjoyed Auckland very much and found the city centre a charming mix of old and new buildings. It is a very green city and best viewed from the Maori hill – an ancient settlement where a only a single tree now stands. Not wishing to spend too much time in the city, we headed south to Rotorua and Whakarewarewa. The roads were fast and there were abundant white crosses at the roadside marking tragic accidents. Had Tom witnessed these he would undoubtedly have been puzzled by the sight. The thought that the newly-invented motor vehicle would have been capable of speeds which could have killed its occupants would have been too fanciful to imagine. And yet, Tom would indeed live through an era when the car developed into a most fabulous form of transport.

TD

Upon reaching this place, a drive of about two or three miles brought us to the hot-springs hotel – a wooden-built house with an iron roof, and situated in the midst of a perfect wilderness, although the grounds close round have been made very attractive, and the fare provided by the landlord was very good. Rain was in full swing here, and of another different kind. No mist. It reminded me of the way sailors put the hose on to us in the mornings when we were going through the tropics; but we were determined that we would lose no time in trying the open-air hot-bath, so under the guidance of the landlord, who had a big lantern – for it was very dark, and nearly 10pm – we started, enveloped in Macintoshes, for the spring and bath. When we got there – or, to be more correct, as we gradually got near – thoughts seemed to arise of what a foolish expedition it was – going to have an open-air hot-bath while it was raining so hard. And then there were such funny noises all round. We could here the sound of water running, and a most unpleasant 'gurgling' kind of sound; and altogether, the only light we had being the rays of the landlord's lantern, the surroundings were peculiar, especially with the terrible downpour of rain. We got used to the 'gurgling' noise before we had been in the district very long, but the first sensations were – well, strange. After about five minutes' walk we came to a wooden shed, which served as a dressing room; and from this by the aid of the lantern, we could just see a bubbling pool. We were soon inside this, and thoroughly enjoyed it. The temperature was about 75 degrees, and the depth a good five feet; The sand at the bottom was quite hot, and the tingling sensation in the lower limbs as the bather sinks to his knees in it is very strange. We got rather wet over the head and shoulders from the rain while swimming about, but that was rather jolly, for it seemed to act as a sort of shower-bath. After arranging our toilet again in the 'dressing room,' the procession re-formed, and we returned to the hotel feeling much refreshed, but anything but at home with the surroundings, which seemed to be nothing but 'gurgling darkness'!

Had to be up very early next morning, as the coach started at eight o'clock, and being of the 'mail' kind, was bound to be punctual. Our destination was perhaps the headquarters of the geyser and hot-spring arrangement, Rotorua, and Whakarewarewa, and well into Maoriland. The musical sound of the Maori language as applied to towns and districts is all very well, but the thing is how to pronounce the names, and remember them after they have been pronounced. We used to bet on them as we came across a good one; but as a rule we were both wrong, and eventually gave it up, for it was tiring work walking round a Maori word three or four times before you could fix it. For instance, in one of the Maori legends there is a chief called Tamatepokaiwhenua, and a pool we passed in our travels went by the name of Te Mimiahomaiterangi! These come fairly easy when you've been in training a bit; but they want some careful handling at first, especially by those who suffer from weakness of the jaws.

Our drive was through about forty miles of country, and a great part of the road was mud. However, the New Zealand coach-horses were good, wiry animals, and are good for forty or fifty miles any day, although twenty is about the average they do. They are very cheap, and run from about 50s to £5 each. At some parts the mud was so bad the coach sank in up to the axles; but the horses worked with a will, and we were landed at the end at registered time. There was not much to see on the way, barring the mud and 'bush'; here and there a squatter's sheep farm could be seen, and now and then a Maori pig; While to me a strange item was the peculiar chattering of strange birds.

We arrived at the Geyser Hotel, Whakarewarewa, just in time for dinner, and quite ready for it, but also very much inclined to walk as lightly as possible, for fear our weight should break through the crust of the earth and send us to explore the hot springs at their base. The 'gurgling' was going on all around, and here and there geysers were shooting up scalding water high into the air, steam was blowing about like smoke from a prairie fire, and altogether we could but think we were treading on 'delicate ground'. Everybody who has been to Whakarewarewa during the last – well, number of years, knows of Sophia, the Maori lady-guide, who takes the money at the entrance to the large area of geysers, and shows you round, explaining how hot this is, how high this water shoots up, etc etc. Sophia is a very shrewd, intelligent, and interesting individual; she has very good manners, can talk well, and is by no means devoid of humour; moreover, she is a bit of a power amongst the tribes. The lady and I got very great friends; perhaps Sophia will forgive me if I say I didn't fall in love with her; she was a good fifty years old, so quite safe, but very charming all the same. I would often leave the hotel, and go and sit by her *whare* and discuss Maori subjects over a smoke. The lady generally used to smoke a pipe, but she would always discard this for a cigarette. The real way to win a Maori's heart is through a packet of cigarettes.

Before leaving this chapter I must really mention the proprietor of the Geyser Hotel, for he was the most extraordinary philosopher I ever met. The son of a Swedish professor, he ran away to sea when a boy, and went through a whole heap of experiences in every corner of the globe until now, at over sixty years of age, he 'bosses' the Geyser. He is a perfect master of fifteen languages, and his occupation previous to hotel proprietorship was that of interpreter and land-purchase agent to the New Zealand Government. He is looked up to as an authority on all Maori matters; and as he has lived amongst them, and almost as one of themselves, for fifteen years, his experience is undoubtedly of a kind called practical. He has his ideas as to the origin of the race, but says that he is contradicted on it at times. He insists that the tribe originally came from the Persian Gulf, and, gradually getting across to the Malay Archipelago, landed at Java and other islands; then, going through the Torres Straits, they got into the Pacific, and amongst the islands there – for, as he points out, they are of the Polynesian race (Shemites). There seems to be a lot in his theory; but, as is known, recognised authorities contradict it, and, as himself points out, the strange part is how they came to miss Australia. However, this is almost too deep a subject for me to go into here.

It needs a Dante to at all adequately describe this hot-spring district; for, setting apart the wonderful sights on every side, of steam and hot water bubbling up a few inches from the earth or shooting high into the air, or the little lakes and fountains of mud, there is that weird and haunting bubbling and gurgling which cannot be seen, and a rumbling as well, which would almost convince one there was a thunderstorm going on deep down in the bowels of the earth. The whole business is so different from anything that is seen in other parts; it has not the awe-inspiring grandeur of Niagara, nor the barbaric splendour of the Rockies; the fairy scenery of Honolulu is absent from it, and so is the picturesque beauty of Samoa. It has a certain fascination about it; but at the same time one cannot help thinking, 'Here is Hades,' and it really only wants the sudden appearance of the gentleman clothed in red, with cloven hoof, barbed tail, and trident, to make the picture complete – in fact, one almost looks for this.

MG

Arriving at Rotorua, the first inkling one has of subterranean activity is the odour. Although not overtly offensive, the sulphurous whiff reminded me of those childhood stink-bombs we used to get in the joke shops. Hot baths were on offer but it was too hot a day to undertake any bathing. This must,

however, be a marvellous winter activity. We then headed to nearby Whakarewarewa which is in the heart of Maoriland. 'Molly' had replaced Tom's 'Sophia' and the Geyser Hotel no longer existed. Nearby, however, the Landmark Hotel/Restaurant still stands.

A small open train takes you round the geysers and hot mud pools. It seemed to me a very strange environment of hissing steam and belching, bubbling, glutinous ooze. It was neither ugly nor beautiful, but rather unworldly, as though the forces of creation were still practising their primeval craft. It did cause dismay to some though, when a mud pool would suddenly bubble up and erupt with scalding steam going everywhere.

The highlight of my visit to New Zealand was undoubtedly a three-day sailing trip on the sailing ketch, *Ketchup*. Fred Grover was the skipper and Maggie and I teamed up with him near Waiheke harbour. The weather was at its most perfect when we set sail. On board was Philip from Canada, who was to prove an excellent chef, and Fred's girlfriend, Dawn. We all gelled well and the trip was a hoot. On the first day we passed the world's largest catamaran *Playstation* (or rather it passed us!) in all its majestic glory. By late afternoon it was time to find a secluded bay to go swimming and diving off the boat.

I had never sailed before and found the whole experience exhilarating. I had never fostered such a good appetite or slept so well in my life. A great sensation of being at one with nature, with good company, great nosh and plenty to drink. I was reluctant to move on but as I drifted off to sleep that night, Khachaturian's haunting adagio of Spartacus rang in my

ears. That had been the signature tune for the 1970's BBC television series, The Onedin Line, which I have forever associated with sailing ships.

The following day we dropped the ladies off at one of Auckland's many piers and then headed further west to dock *Ketchup*. As Fred and Philip dropped the sails the atmosphere changed gear into a much more industrious mode. As the diesel engine spluttered into a rattling, smoky drone, it became obvious from Fred's glancing and searching looks, that not all was shipshape.

I got the message.

We set to and cleaned the vessel from top to bottom. I could not believe we could have filled so many bin bags with garbage of the clinking variety. On disembarking a gleaming *Ketchup* I could not help but compare its required upkeep as being akin to the high standards of housekeeping at Scotch whisky distilleries.

The ladies had been shopping in our absence and my last night in New Zealand was made special by their preparations – deliciously fresh seafood, local wines and of course natural conversation.

I observed they were great connoisseurs of not just Scotch but also tea and in particular Lipton's tea. I could not refrain from telling one of Tom's stories when he was big-game hunting in Africa. Tom was a great friend of the 'tea baron' Thomas Lipton and wrote to his bachelor friend about his findings. In his letter he observed that you could 'buy two wives here, for a packet of Lipton's Tea' – a swift reply from London followed – 'have sent samples of tea, please send samples of wives.'

The banter continued and I learned on this trip that married couples who are having a quarrel is known as having a 'domestic'. That if one is spouting verbal diarrhoea in this part of the world you are kindly reminded to shut the **** up!'

I left this marvellous place with spirits wonderfully lifted and headed by plane the following day for Sydney. From this point on, I would be travelling homewards.

CHAPTER 5

AUSTRALIA, HONG KONG, SHANGHAI AND HOME

SYDNEY

FIFTH week on the hop. The constant changing of addresses and time zones was starting to take its toll. Modern-day travel can be a debilitating experience.

It was now well into January and on arrival at Sydney I was hit by a wall of heat. Tom describes this most effectively and had it not been for the cooling breeze wafting off Sydney Harbour, it would have been insufferable. Sydney is, however, a wonderful city and a five-minute stroll from my hotel took me to the Opera House overlooking perhaps the most beautiful harbour in the world. Tom's route differed from mine slightly but he had much to say about this part of the world.

TD

We left Melbourne at five o'clock in the afternoon; and at 11pm, just when every one was thoroughly tired and ready to 'turn in', we had to 'turn out'. This was at a place called Albury, just on the borders of New South Wales; and as Victoria goes in for the narrow gauge railways, and New South Wales patronises the broad gauge system, a change here is inevitable. Why on earth the two colonies cannot go in for the same thing, and so save everyone the bother and nuisance of being hustled out just when they are ready to go to sleep, I cannot make out. Perhaps when that much-to-be-desired result, Imperial Federation, becomes an accomplished fact, these little details will receive attention, and the journey between Melbourne and Sydney will be robbed of its greatest inconvenience and worst annoyance.

The New South Wales part of the passage, though, was very comfortable, for the carriages were 'Pullman'. At eleven next morning we arrived at Sydney; but, really, from the heat I thought that the engine driver had altered the route, and taken us to another destination. I was quite prepared to find a little heat in Sydney, but not quite as much as there really was, for it was awful. It puzzled me how water could be kept from boiling, or meat from being cooked. I didn't try it, but I am quite sure if I had stuck a slice of bread in the sun, it would have been toast in no time.

The houses give off the heat tremendously, and the pavements are like hot bricks; if the free-spitting Americans were about, one would see nothing but little phizzing geysers all over the pavement. Even the asphalt is soft, and retains the impression of one's boots, as well as sometimes the heel of the boot. No, I did not like Sydney; it was too hot, far too hot. Otherwise, it was not half a bad place, although the huge donkey-engine pulling a clumsy-looking lot of carriages up the middle of the street – playing at steam-tramways as it were – looks so ridiculous. This must be dangerous for traffic; for, although a man stands at the corner of streets with a big red flag to warn anyone coming along, horses are sensitive creatures, and object to red flags, just as they do to other things of a peculiar nature calculated to upset any one's highly-strung nerves.

Melbourne is far ahead of Sydney in the matter of streets; but Sydney Harbour, or, to be more correct, Port Jackson, is simply magnificent from a picturesque point of view. Botany Bay is close handy – a name which conjures up all manner of visions of the old convict days, for here the members of the firm of Bill Sykes and Co. of the period were sent in very large numbers for a change of air, but unfortunately many innocent persons were included in the shipments. The university, which stands in a domain of some 150 acres, is the most important building in the whole of the Australasian Colonies, and indeed there are few to beat it in the Mother Country. Churches are very plentiful, and so are public houses. There are several theatres, hospitals, etc, etc, and 'larrikinism' holds its own. The people of Sydney are no doubt pretty well accustomed to this most objectionable feature of life in their city, but to a stranger it is absolutely detestable.

A surprise awaited me in Sydney in connection with my irrepressible Yankee friend, for he had struck out in a new line altogether. He had gone mad on music, and the long-named Italians he spoke of was something appalling, and indeed to my non-musical ear sounded very bad. I thought at first he had contracted the very bad Australian habit of using wicked words, but was assured he only spoke of composers, musicians, and artists, so I was agreeably relieved. But the surprise was, for the sake of amusement – the steamer mania having set him on – he had arranged to take a concert party round New Zealand etc. He had intended going to Japan, but thought it would be too cold on arriving there. The enthusiasm with which he described and eulogised his company was most amusing – and such a company! Yes, yes, we had a private concert in order to test the individual merits of the members, and then the whole of the artists were assembled together. Savile Row had certainly not been the address of the tailors who fitted any of them out, and in some cases the apparel wore a look of vacancy, as though the memory as to who its modeller had been had faded away. But the gentlemen, if not over-careful as to their clothing and finger-nails, were most particular in the arrangement of their long and somewhat greasy locks, and through constant practice had acquired a noble artistic finish in the manner in which they gracefully passed their fingers through their sleeky hair, in order to keep it in position. They were also more partial to clay pipes than cigars, and certainly seemed more at home with them. I presume all these little peculiarities were but signs of talent, so I must not jest about them, for talent in any form is always to be commended.

As I really couldn't stand the heat of Sydney, I didn't stay there long, and, after having a good look round the place, got on the move once more and started for Hong Kong.

MG

Nearby the opera house, by the water's edge I spotted an oyster bar with an outside terrace. Sterling was very strong and a dozen fleshy oysters cost me about £6 – not bad, even if there were no pearls inside them! There was not much eating in these slippery fellows so I succumbed to half-a-dozen fat langoustines as a dessert. They had been stir-fried in garlic, olive oil and lemon juice and were delicious washed down with a cold Chardonnay. The sun was slowly disappearing across the harbour and I felt very much at ease with my lot. A peaceful night's sleep back at the hotel completed the day.

The following day I decided to go on a two-hour cruise around the harbour: probably the best way to see the sights, and certainly the coolest. The trip on *Vagabond Majestic* takes you right out to South Head where the harbour joins the ocean. Along the way many sheltered and secluded bays offer naturists the opportunity to reveal all, but be assured that I did not expose my well-honed Elgin physique to the locals!

Again Hilton Hotels were very kind to me during my short stay in Sydney and the hotel was ideally situated in the heart of the city. Nearby, the Sydney Town Hall was host to the Proms and my last night was memorable. I took myself off to see 'Hands On' which was to prove a masterful showcase to the skills of six Ukrainian pianists and it only cost a fiver to get in! The works of Chopin, Handel, Rachmaninov and Stravinsky filled a very enjoyable evening.

If only the heat could be turned down a little, this would be an idyllic city in which to live; everyone seems to be full of life. It was therefore with much regret that I left Sydney, but I vowed to return and see it properly in the future.

The Sydney to Hong Kong flight awaited me the next day and I was impressed by the level of service on the Qantas 747. Although it was a longer flight than I had expected, at nearly eight hours, the tasty food and in-flight films broke up the journey.

*   *   *

HONG KONG

TD

The voyage to Hong Kong! – Yes, it was a voyage and no mistake, and it was also an experience I have no wish to repeat. But of that later on. The name of the boat I went by was the SS ………*. Well, it was a name I shall long remember; but, with the terrors of the libel law rising before me, I will

*Saghalien

refrain from mentioning it. I heard of a bankrupt once living in a grand style in a huge mansion kept up by his wife's money, and who, in a way to appease his creditors, invited them all to a musical evening; they went; he sang 'You'll Remember Me', and there was an almost unanimous chorus of 'We'll never forget you'. That's how I feel about this boat.

From Sydney to the Heads, the entrance to the harbour – Port Jackson – is about an hour's run, but the view in steaming down is really magnificent, while the harbour itself is as fine a one as any in the world. As 'Frisco and as Melbourne, it is natural and land-locked; but, good as I had thought the two former, they paled immeasurably before the grand, the unique, the magnificent harbour of Port Jackson.

The hour's run down to the Heads is anything but an uninteresting passage, for the scenery on both sides is most attractive, and keeps the mind well occupied during the whole time. There are sharks, too, in Port Jackson, and not in small numbers either – in fact one would almost think it was a kind of headquarters in the shark world. I spent the time steaming down admiring the scenery, keeping my eye on the water, wondering if anyone would tumble overboard to give the sharks a treat, and also let other people see how sharks behaved as soon as they heard the cry 'Man Overboard!' This didn't come off, though, so I am still ignorant as to the behaviour of this kind of fish under peculiar circumstances.

Out once more on the open sea, the breeze comes with most refreshing delightfulness after the intense and suffocating heat of Sydney, and although it may be a bit rough, the change is grand, for one feels that at least it is possible to breath.

Now, however, began that month's experience, which I never want again.

The assortment of travellers was varied in the extreme, including both those who had and those who had not paid their passage. Fourteen days before sailing I had booked a cabin which was said to be the best on the ship and next to the captain's. However, at the last moment I was advised by the manager of the company to exchange into another which had just been forfeited, as it was so much better than the one I had originally selected.

I changed.

On retiring to rest, I began to think what an excellent article a boy John Chinaman was, for the one told off to look after me had laid out my sleeping attire most carefully.

I began to unrobe. Coming to my necktie, I threw it down, and it went on to the floor; but it didn't lie still. No, it moved most perceptibly. Watching to discern the cause, my eye came in contact with a movement on the part of the left leg of my pyjamas so carefully laid out. This was very strange – and yes, my pyjama jacket made a movement as though it had heaved a sigh. Then the necktie moved again *en bloc* at least an inch, and there was a disagreeable noise about – not loud, but a sort of filling-the-air, ghostlike kind of noise. Then something crawled over my stockingless foot, and gave me a shock. Cockroaches! Yes, cockroaches in swarms and not the common or garden kind of little insects so well known to Britishers. Oh dear no! Cockroaches of a size that would make the ordinary kitchen black beetle think himself a dwarf – tropical cockroaches that grow in size as the heat gets greater; and they were present in crowds!

After putting on my slippers, and executing a wild war dance over the floor, each step being accompanied by a crunch and a swish, I perceived the endeavour to lessen the multitude was in vain, so I resigned myself to the inevitable, and slept. Yes, I slept, dreaming that I was a Maori chief ruling over the destinies of a large country, which was a kind of amalgamation of Fiji, the Highlands of Scotland, Seven Dials, American Prairie, Sydney and New Zealand geysers, and that all my subjects were cockroaches, beetles, and snakes. But my rest was not for long, neither were my dreams to be undisturbed.

After reaching a point where a military tournament was being held in a stalactite cave of huge proportions, and a grand tug-of-war was going on between fourteen snakes of immense length and 173 Brobdingnagian cockroaches, I awoke with a start, and the impression that a steeplechase of some kind was being held on the floor of my cabin. I was not far wrong, for upon getting my matchbox from under the pillow, and striking a light, I beheld a by no means small assembly of rats. I knew they were rats from their shape; but from the size anyone might have been excused for mistaking them for well-grown Ostend rabbits. The light startled them, and their conclave was suddenly adjourned, the one I took to be chairman of the meeting making a hasty dive for somewhere, and disappearing. The rest followed his example with all speed, and once more I slept.

MG

I was curious to visit Hong Kong again. At the time of writing, this former British colony had reverted to full Chinese sovereignty. I described my first impressions of Hong Kong in *A Nip Around The World* and in spite of this major development, not much had changed in the interim. Hong Kong is now a Special Administrative Region (SAR) of the Peoples Republic of China, and the handover is now a fading news story. There is not a jackboot in sight in any respect. There is a new flag and a new leader, who takes the title 'Chief Executive' not 'Governor' which in itself is more commercially revealing. The latter term reminds me of an authoritative bully in an orphanage! These aspects aside, the changes seem to be for the better and the direst predictions from the multitudes of journalists have not materialised. The rock is still a key trading centre and financial capital and will welcome 60 million tourists annually in the next century. Why on earth would any style of government wish to change this? A sad loss to the UK, a golden goose for China.

TD

Watching from the bridge of the rat and cockroach-laden boat as she neared the harbour of Hong Kong, the gradually developing scenery attracted greater and greater attention, until, at the time the anchor was dropped, the scene was one that only a painter or a poet could adequately describe. Imagine a high background of rock, half barren and half studded with trees, and, rising in terraces amongst this, good-looking and substantially-built residences, some in rows and some dotted here and there, a foreground of a magnificent sheet of water, with the blue rippling waves dancing and sparkling in the sunshine, a crowd of shipping, consisting of merchantmen, men-of-war, passenger boats, and mail steamers. Steam launches darting here and there and everywhere, with their screeching whistles going all over the place, the rough business-like appearance of the whole being pleasantly broken by quaint Chinese junks flitting hither and thither, and a goodly collection of the almost clumsy-looking sampan, and there you have some idea of the view of Hong Kong, after passing through the famous Ly-ce-moon Pass. As a Portuguese captain exclaimed, it was a sight to give anyone an idea of England's power in colonising; but, apart from that, quaintness, novelty and thorough picturesqueness all lend themselves to give an additional charm to the scene.

It is finely situated, and makes a capital naval station for the East, while its value as a commercial centre is increasing each day. There is a strong contrast to the islands round about, which are under Portuguese sway, for in these things are in such a wretched state they have advanced scarcely one iota since they were occupied some three hundred years ago.

Our boat did not anchor close up to the quay, so we had to be taken off in sampans, and the short trip from the vessel to the shore gave me an insight of a very peculiar part of Chinese life – the manners and customs of the floating population. The boat was not much more than twenty feet long, and though I did not measure, I should say its depth would not be more than two feet, or its beam over five feet, and yet it was not only used as a means of conveyance, but it was the domicile, home, and family mansion of the owner, his wife, and family of three children! We heard that the previous night two men had been suffocated in such a similar hold, the cold being so intense they had shut themselves in, but that such things were by no means of any uncommon occurrence – and I can quite believe it.

The forepart of these boats is decked over, and this forms the 'house' – certainly not a commodious domain, for the measurement couldn't possibly be more than five feet by four; but John doesn't mind, and it doesn't seem to matter to him how many youngsters are about. During my stay I saw more than one boat where the children numbered five and six! I heard – and believe it is correct – that there are over 20,000 Chinese living entirely in these boats and junks in Hong Kong harbour. It is hardly comprehensible to a Britisher that such could be the case, but it is so.

My first night in Hong Kong – it was the end of January – happened to be the coldest (so the people said) ever experienced, and yet the thermometer only went down to 26°. My, how people did complain of the cold in the morning! To tell the truth, though, I joined them, and was well to the front in my grumbling; but then there was an excuse for me, because only two days before I had been sweltering in 95° – rather a sudden drop. I couldn't quite make out how it was all the Chinese people looked so stout, until it was explained to me, and someone said, 'Man, they can't walk for clothes.' It appears that as the weather gets colder, these interesting and ingenious people just stick on another suit of clothes – if that be the correct term to apply to the wonderful arrangements with which they clothe themselves – and there they leave them until the warm weather turns up again. It often happens that a Chinaman will be carrying his whole wardrobe on his back. Curious people!

The island is very mountainous, although so small, and Victoria Peak, the highest point, has an altitude of somewhere about 1,825 feet. Of course the proper thing to do is to go to the top of this, so, wishing to be always proper, I ascended. I wasn't sorry when I had reached the top, and my thanksgiving was fervent when I was once more on the level of the sea.

You don't walk up, neither do you ride on donkeys or mules; a cable car is the conveyance that takes you up, and it seems more like going up a great height in a lift, with the sides out, so that you can see all round. It is decidedly not the kind of recreation I should advise to anyone of a nervous temperament, or anyone whose appetite suddenly disappears at the sight of the matutinal frizzled bacon. Still, although the ascent is made by means of such an almost vertical tram, it is worth the fright when the summit is reached, for the picture all round is a perfectly grand one. In the air, at an elevation of about a third of a mile; below is seen the whole of the island, but most distinctly the splendid harbour of Hong Kong, with its crowds of shipping. On every hand is the sea, while away to the north is the mainland of China itself. It is really a glorious sight, and such a one as perhaps it is impossible to see elsewhere.

We were 'chaired' to a very fair restaurant, in order that we might try a real, genuine Chinese dinner. With a heroism worthy of far greater deeds, I stuck to my guns, and went through the whole lot of courses, although at times I must say I nearly gave in. The hedgehog soup was very passable, but I can't say I quite relished the boiled owl with beetle sauce; the fricasseed kittens were not at all bad, but I soon left off when the stewed puppy dog was put in front of me. I had a try at it, though, just to say I had some. It is not a dish I should encourage my friends to try, although they might do worse than get familiar with grilled horse steak. We did try that peculiarly Chinese epicurean dish 'blind mice,' and I don't think I should care to do so either. They call this 'Milhi,' which really means 'mice'; they are placed alive on a small tray before each guest, who, taking them one by one by the tail, dips them in honey, then swallows them! It is said that when the Emperor's wedding was celebrated a few years ago, 50,000 of these young mice were consumed at the banquet!

MG

My only night in Hong Kong City was in all admission, a self-indulgence. I stayed at the Peninsula (The Pen) in Tsim Sha Tsui on the southern tip of the Kowloon peninsula. The hotel is 70 years old and is one of the grand old travel hotels of the world. The Pen has played host to Noel Coward and various 'James Bonds' and yes, you can get a vodka martini 'shaken not stirred'. The sea-view rooms offer delightful vistas across Hong Kong Island and Victoria Harbour to the south. One peculiarity is the upper floor urinals which also offer splendid views – indeed I am told the gents are open to all sexes for an hour each evening to allow the ladies to sample the magnificent views – across the harbour, that is! The Star Ferry takes you swiftly across Hong Kong Harbour (which means 'fragrant harbour' in Cantonese). This historic ferry which is 100 years old this year, whisks nearly 100,000 passengers to and from Hong Kong Island every day.

I took my lunch at the East Lake Restaurant which was bustling with noisy Chinese. I loved the atmosphere and my heaped plate of chilli clams was soon replenished with deep-fried squid, Chinese mushrooms and vegetable fried rice which I washed down with the local beer.

The Peak Tram is a must, and I enjoyed it as much as my first visit in 1995. The view from Victoria Peak is stunning. Again about 100 years old, the tram which seems to climb and descend almost vertically, must have been a relief to the labourers of 1888, who once carried over-stuffed 'gweilos' (foreign devils) to the summit in sedan chairs and rickshaws.

My last night in Hong Kong was spent at the new airport terminal – the Royal Airport Hotel at Chek Lap Kok. The hotel had just opened when I arrived and was going through the 'teething stages'. On checking in I was offered a voucher which entitled me to a complimentary welcome drink of beer, home wine or non-alcoholic beverage. On presenting this at the bar I received another ticket which read, *'Please bear with us, we regret that we are unable to serve alcoholic drinks until the granting of our Liquor Licence'*. Why, I thought, did they offer a voucher in the first place? This, however, did not reflect badly on the rest of the hotel and I enjoyed my last night in Hong Kong very much. The airport itself is a mass of polished steel and glass and is not my idea of an airport, but it is probably considered state-of-the-art by those in the know. However, I did discover a tiny Irish bar on the ground floor which was serving at 7am. A full Irish breakfast 'cheerer' was duly ordered and heartily consumed.

The following morning I arose excited with the prospect of my early flight – Eastern China Airlines to Shanghai. This was to be the last leg of my round-the-world journey. It did not quite cover Tom's entire route of 1898-1899 but it was a pretty good shot.

* * *

SHANGHAI

Culture shock. Shanghai. The very name conjures up frenetic images in the mind and I was to enjoy every minute of my stay. The most striking point on entering the city is the sheer volume of people, most of them careering around on bicycles. Everything, including the kitchen sink, is carried on these vehicles.

TD

Shanghai is on the Woosung River, before entering which a rather awkward 'bar' has to be crossed, and there are times when some steamers cannot get across unless the tide is high. As luck would have it, we were not detained outside, owing to an accident that had happened about two months previously. A steamer was run down, and sunk in midstream on this bar, making such a rush of water one side that the waterway had been deepened by four feet or more.

On landing, our impressions were very good, for the aspect of the place was thoroughly business-like and prosperous. As usual, we found a big river population, the number being put down at from 12,000 to 15,000. Like in other Eastern places, the Europeans here seem to have the knack of making themselves comfortable and building good houses, for the private residences as well as the clubs are all that possibly could be desired. The Shanghai Club is the principal one, and it really is a marvel. It is the meeting place of the European business-men; and about twelve o'clock, midday, all the offices are closed, and the majority of the people go to the club, which is for the time being a kind of Exchange. The members are a very jolly set of fellows, and I soon felt quite at home there.

It was cold here, colder than even the oldest inhabitant could remember, and so it ought to be, for 10 below zero is all very well now and then, but to have it as a regular thing every winter would get very monotonous. There was a lot of snow as well, and a number of large lumps of ice were drifting down the river.

Of course I went to the Chinese City, and was very much surprised at the reception I got there, for, from one or two things I had read, and a few more I had heard, I quite expected the chances of my returning in anything but a battered condition were very few but – of course putting aside the questions of smells, which I must say almost equalled those of Canton – really I did not meet with the slightest incivility from any one.

My experience was that the natives seemed only too pleased if you took notice of their work. Quaint, very quaint, were some of the parts of the place, as were also the stuffy little workshops. In one shop, about ten or twelve feet square, I counted eleven workmen – tailors, tinsmiths, shoemakers, etc – all trades were represented in these small shops – and the workmen seemed very comfortable. One reason of this is, there are no trades unions or large monopolies. In many cases, I found the master gave his men, who were generally relatives, an interest in the work, lived with them under the same roof, and fed with them out of the same bowl of rice – in fact, each establishment seemed to be a family concern. The gorgeous mandarin, however, is the lord of creation among them, and he takes the pool.

MG

The Shanghai Hilton (surprise, surprise) was to be my home base for the next few days. The concierge could not have been more helpful and advised me to hire a local guide and car to see the city proper. This was to prove a good move as the city is vast, and many of the places of interest are well off the beaten track. The weather was dry but cold at around freezing point and we set off to visit the Jade Buddha Temple. This was to prove a colourful and mystical experience. The air was full of incense from ember-tipped joss sticks. The ritual of lighting these was similar to candle burning in European churches. The Chinese bow gently in front of towering gold-gilt Buddhas clutching many smouldering sticks. I felt I was intruding in this very private and thoughtful place. Tiled pagodas dating back to the 15th century cast huge shadows over the proceedings and a chilling breeze hastened our departure.

TD

Just before completing my round of the city, I thought my last hour had arrived, for all at once a most frightful noise arose about twenty yards in front of me; a bonfire was also lighted, and upon this, boxes, boots, papers – in fact, all manner of things were being thrown. 'Here', thought I, 'is another occasion when discretion should for a time take the place of valour. I will return by another way. I do not mind being drowned at sea during my travels, smashed in a railway accident, devoured by Japanese land-crabs, or having this mortal coil shuffled from off me by any such romantic means; but never, never will I be frizzled by a Chinaman!' Thinking thus, I was upon the point of retracing my steps when my guide stopped me. Was he in the plot as well? Should I brain him and fly? My fears – no, not my fears, because I was not afraid; no, my determination was altered – that's better – by the soothing tones of the gentle Chinee, as he pointed to the place and said, 'Ah! one piecee man hab catchee die!' I thought as he hadn't caught me, the 'piecee man' could catch just whatever he liked; but I found out after, that the meaning of the phrase was that a man had died! Yes, so it was; a man had died and in order to propitiate, or 'Chin-Chin' the Joss to send his soul somewhere where it would be comfortable, all this noise was being made. The *paid* mourners, wrapped in sackcloth, were lying in the gutter wallowing in all the filth – wailing, moaning, and groaning to such an extent that I got fairly bewildered, so went off without waiting to see the finish of the performance.

Like Canton and other Chinese cities, this Chinese part of Shanghai is walled in with an enormously thick and high wall, in which are, I think, seven great gates that are shut and guarded at night. By the way, a wholesale wine merchant in the English settlement told me that a Chinaman made the best of all warehousemen in a wine merchant's establishment, not only because they did not drink very much, but that if they did, any one could always tell, for half a glass of wine, or anything intoxicating, caused a large red ring to appear round his eyes, and by looking at him and counting the rings, it was possible to find out just exactly how much he had imbibed. Very ingenious this! I had never heard of it before; but I suppose it's true. I know that the age of a tree or a cow can be told by looking at the rings of the trunk or the horn, but this way of telling how much a man has had to drink was quite new to me. It would be a good thing sometimes if this were the case with Englishmen, and would assist most materially in 'drunk and disorderly' cases. Imagine a man denying before a magistrate at Bow Street that he had been drunk; how easy it would be for His Worship to say, 'Constable, did you examine his eyes?' 'Yes, your wusship; but the rings all round each eye were so mixed up over 'is nose, and went right under the 'air of 'is 'ead, we couldn't count how many there really was!' 'Ten shillings or seven days!' Why the whole thing would be as easy as ABC.

Leaving Shanghai in the tender in order to get outside the bar to board the *Empress of India*, although there was some fog about, looking at the banks of the river every evidence could be seen of the Chinaman's industry, for there hardly seemed an inch of ground that was not cultivated. It is said that the Chinese make the best gardeners in the world, and from what I saw, I should really think this was correct; in fact, I almost agreed with those people who called Shanghai the 'Garden of China.' Of course, I had not seen much of the Celestial Empire; but it must be something very good indeed to beat what I saw here.

MG

I loved the Yayaan Garden which is an excellent model of classical Chinese gardening. It was built in 1559 during the reign of Ming Emperor Jaijing as a private garden. Countless goldfish gently swim in shoals through the interconnecting ponds. With an area over two hectares, the garden is famous for a number of architectural marvels, including the 'Big Rockery', the naturally hollowed 'Jade Boulder', the Hall of an Emerald Touch of Spring, the 'Inner Garden' and countless other cultural relics.

A walk along the Bund beside the River Huangpu finished my day trip. Here stands the magnificent Shanghai Bank. Inside it, marvellous frescos depicting the major capitals of the world may be seen, but you are not allowed to photograph them.

China is one of the last bastions of the Marxist communist ethic but I, as a Westerner, did not in the least way feel intimidated by this. I found the city 'western' in many ways and major multinational companies have satellites here, among them Siemens and Volkswagen. Also, Irish bars are numerous! The food was part of my enjoyment and not dissimilar to good Chinese restaurants back home. One delicacy I had not experienced was fried scorpion which I found quite like shrimp. Another, which may disturb some readers, was 'live' monkey brain, but I will not expand on that. I did not try it, but it is supposed to be delicious washed down with rice wine.

My last night in Shanghai was accompanied by Nancy from the Hilton. She worked on the top-storey cocktail bar which overlooks the sprawling city. The staff here all have western names which I thought a bit of a shame. Nancy's real name sounded much more exotic – Zhang. She

proved a marvellous companion and ambassador for the city and we visited many pubs. I particularly liked 'Rogers' Beer Keller on three floors with live, albeit western music. To finish off we visited Flanagan's, and found the Guinness to be as good as it gets.

On rising the next day I was to receive a shock. On opening my bedroom curtains, 27 storeys up, two very cheeky Chinese boys waved me a good morning. They were both suspended on a very rickety-looking platform from above, but were none the worse for it during their window-cleaning duties. I waved back, then suddenly remembered I was in my birthday suit!

My journey now would take me back to Hong Kong to connect up with a British Airways flight to London Heathrow. My six weeks were up. Tom would take a further voyage of six weeks to return to London, where he expressed to feeling wonderful. My passage to Heathrow did not quite have the same allure but the feeling of returning home at last was mutual.

*   *   *

HOME

TD

It seemed strange, after knocking about so much, seeing so many different countries, and knowing that there was still a six or seven weeks' voyage ahead, that I was going home at last. That word home sounds very different on different occasions, and this was one of the times when the full meaning comes strongly to the front. Here was I, considerably over 10,000 miles from the British Isles, starting to 'go home,' and as I thought of it, visions of Old England and Bonnie Scotland rose up, and I must confess I felt rather like I used to at school at the end of term, when I left school and started on my way home to spend my holidays in the best way I could.

I always used to enjoy those holidays, more so than the rest of the family, I believe. There were certain neighbours, too, who never seemed to look on those holidays with pleasure. One in particular, I remember, who didn't like them, and only just because I would at times get up early in the morning and try my hand at reducing the game and vermin in the district. Most ridiculous, I thought at the time (but I can understand it now), because I didn't kill much. He said that was just it; in fact his words were: 'It isn't what he kills, it's what the little devil frightens away that I object to'. Ah me, many is the gamekeeper in the neighbourhood who has tried not only to frighten the 'little devil' away, but to get him in his terrible grip. It was a great nuisance being bothered by these men so, because I wasn't a poacher – only an amateur sportsman. Still there are some people who will not see any idea different to the one fixed in their own mind. More than once, I verily believe, I should have been most ignominiously removed by these objectionable gentlemen, had it not been for my most faithful red dog, who had the same rooted antipathy to gamekeepers as myself, and could smell them a mile off, and so give me warning that perhaps it would be as well to change the base of our operations. Well, the 'going home for the holidays' kind of feeling came over me as I stepped on board the *Saghalien*, and I almost felt inclined to shout, but on second thoughts came to the conclusion that it would be hardly the correct thing to do...

So far, on the voyage, when touching at different places, we had been spared the ordeal of custom-house examination; but now we were fairly in for it, for all our luggage would be turned out, and I had *six* portmanteaux. When I was on shore, standing in fear and trembling by my baggage, wondering what would be the result of the examination, and how long it would take me to repack everything after it had been upset, three gentlemen approached me and most politely raised their hats. I saw they were officials of some sort, so, to be equally polite, I bowed and raised my hat. Bowing again, and pointing to my baggage, one asked, 'Tabac?' I bowed and said, 'No.' 'Speerits?' 'No'; and imagine my surprise when my things were chalked, and I was free! The polite French gentlemen were customs-house officers! Fancy a British Exciseman raising his hat or bowing, or a railway booking clerk saying 'Sir,' or 'Madam'! Such things are not in our country; but why they should not be, I do not know. Some people have an insane notion that it is foolish to be polite to all classes, but I stoutly oppose this notion. I have travelled now all over the world, and in some very peculiar quarters; but by being polite to all, and treating people as I found them, I can safely say the cases of incivility I have met with could be counted on one hand, and that then there would be fingers to spare.

At Dover the almost ludicrous, but at first surprising, thing is to get London papers the day they are issued! Weeks old had been the usual thing for so long, that to see the actual date on the paper, and know it had only been just issued, caused at first a most peculiar sensation. Heaps of papers were bought by everyone just to see the date; but, leaving Dover, and getting into the regular English country, more peculiar feelings still arose, and it seemed as though I had been to sleep for months and months *à la* Rip Van Winkle, or as a hungry man would feel when placed in front of a substantial meal. All round are the neatly kept hedgerows, the old familiar fields, the truly rustic spots so well known to all lovers of country life; the hop-poles and hop-fields of Kent; the open villages, happy in the security of a free country, minus the walls and guards to which the eye of the foreign traveller becomes accustomed; and, in fact, on every hand are signs of peace, of happiness, and of prosperity that not only make one's breast swell with pardonable pride, but ejaculate with heartfelt earnestness, 'Thank God I am a Britisher!'

The train speeds away through the sweet green fields of Old England, and signs of approaching town are seen. These signs get more and more distinct, and familiar landmarks come in sight; the suburbs are reached and passed, the towers of Westminster rise to view, the Thames is crossed; and then, indeed, at home at last, for Charing Cross is reached. Here are friends to greet me, and, vigilant as ever, my old valet Dobson, who has since passed away to that land from which there is no return.

Here once more I stand in London, dear old London, home again safe and well. The smart, quick, and businesslike Customs officers, although so different from the Frenchmen, get through their work; and once more I go out into the streets of the greatest and most marvellous city on this earth, to be assailed with the true London cries that fall almost as music on the returned wanderer's ear, 'Piccadilly, 'Yde Park, 'Ammersmith,' 'Paper – extira speshul, all the winners,' and the old familiar cries, and to see once more the bustle and rush which is simply unequalled in its genuineness! Yes, I am at home once more; and the substantial superiority over everything I have seen, which seems to pervade the very air, comes before me like a flash.

Republics, kingdoms, empires, all are good; but Old England beats the lot, and London (ignoring Macaulay) says as with Tennyson in The Brook:

Men may come, and men may go,
But I go on for ever.

CHAPTER 6

TALKING SPIRITS

I had a dream...

MG

'Well Tom, here we are one hundred years on. What changes? What advances? Things really move fast now. Air travel has just about killed off the ocean liners and railways you were used to, although some of them are still around.'

TD

'Malcolm, you certainly followed my footsteps at a gallop. That 747 jumbo jet is a great beast of a bird and fast too. But Concorde...simply unbelievable! *Titanic* was the fastest way across the Atlantic in my time, and thank God I missed it by a squeak – but it was tempting, I can tell you! All that pomp and luxury, well, for some of us at least. And of course back then two of my fellow Scots – John Logie Baird and Alexander Graham Bell – were developing a couple of things called telephone and television. Did they take off?'

MG

'That's an understatement Tom. Most of the developed world uses the telephone for day-to-day communication and television exists in almost every home in the developed world. In fact, the portable mobile phones can now be seen just about everywhere. We are in the age of the personal computer, E-mail and the Internet which allow us to communicate with practically anyone in the world, in seconds, at minimal cost, via telephone lines and satellites orbiting the earth in space.'

TD

'Satellites? Good Lord! Who would have thought…it all sounds amazing. As you well know Malcolm, I was a firm advocate of advertising. Remember my Dewarisms? "ADVERTISE OR FOSSILISE" or "ADVERTISING IS TO BUSINESS WHAT IMAGINATION IS TO POETRY" to quote a few! Can you advertise on these machines?'

MG

'Of course you can. The television is one of the strongest mediums for persuasive advertising. Surprisingly enough, only recently has Scotch

whisky started to advertise on television in the UK. I think if you had been around, this would have been quite different! The Internet is also ideal, in that you can create 'websites'. These hold information/advertising for your products and the user simply logs onto your unique site. It is world-wide, easily accessed and there are no geographical barriers or boundaries to worry about.'

TD

'There must be a hell of a lot of cables and telegraph wires going round the world!'

MG

'Well, yes and no Tom. Of course there are millions of miles of cables, all sending and receiving communications, but the great breakthrough was made quite recently. The development of the microchip and space satellites has changed the face of communications forever. I don't want to become too technical Tom, but in a nutshell these satellites are rocketed into space by

means of high-octane propellant and placed in orbit around the earth. They serve millions of people around the world by bouncing signals from the planet back to locations on the other side of the world. It's a sort of electronic semaphore.'

TD
'Why yes, something like that was first used by *Titanic* to send distress signals in 1912. By the way, what is high-octane propellant?'

MG
'Correct, but the tiny microchip, smaller than a lady's fingernail can process information, which previously required vast data storage machines. They can easily be sent out to space as vital components on communications satellites. High-octane fuel is a derivative of the fuels you would have seen used on early motor cars. Like whisky, it is distilled to intensify its strength and concentrate its power!'

TD
'Travel and technology have certainly advanced beyond belief – there will soon be a man on the moon!'

MG
'Sorry Tom, but that happened in 1969. He was an American by the name of Neil Armstrong.'

TD

'Ah well, at least he had a good Scots name! To change the subject Malcolm, in my time, women were starting to get their point across. I noticed this and commented upon it: "WE SEE MORE AND MORE OF WOMEN EVERY YEAR" and "TODAY WOMEN DISPLAY MORE BACKBONE THAN MEN".'

MG
'Yes Tom, women have come to the forefront in society, although there are still prejudices. In business, politics, music, and the professions they have thrived – but we need to see more of them. One phenomenon, and I don't want to bring religion into this, just an observation, is that a recent invention – the contraceptive pill, has given women more freedom of choice. They are no longer chained to the kitchen sink, no-one should be, but sadly this persists, particularly in the under-developed countries.

On this last point, the world has hardly changed at all. Half the world is still on, or below the poverty line. There is now the 'rich' industrialised world and the 'poor' under-developed world. Serious poverty and malnutrition still persist – nothing much changes.'

TD
'On my travels Malcolm, cash was such a bother. Sending letters to arrange withdrawals, making appointments with bankers to collect sums of foreign currency was an annoyance. We often carried large amounts of cash, which was risky in itself.'

MG

'That has all changed. For my trip in your footsteps, I carried two plastic cards. In effect they were cards of guaranteed credit. In all the places I visited, from Chicago to Fiji to Shanghai, all I had to do was to visit an 'autoteller'. These are automated 'safes' usually sited in public places and owned and serviced by the banks and credit card companies.

I simply inserted my unique card, entered a code number known only to me, press for the amount required and the machine delivered the cash, in the currency of the country I was in.'

TD

'Amazing Malcolm, what convenience and security. Is this service expensive?'

MG

'No, not at all. Of course there are some transaction costs, but provided you keep in credit and pay your monthly bills on time, the cost is minimal.'

TD

'Did the motor car eventually supersede the horse and carriage?'

MG

Yes, but the huge volume of motor cars on the roads now has caused major problems. This is mainly in the major cities with much congestion and pollution.'

TD

'Surely not as bad as the 'Pea Souper' London smog? That used to give me terrible bronchitis'

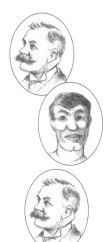

MG

'We are far more aware of those problems today and the implications for our health. It is actually illegal to burn coal in many city centres these days.'

TD

'On my journeys, keeping in good health was always a great concern – there were many serious and deadly diseases about: cholera, typhoid, and smallpox to name a few. I could not visit Vancouver Island because of a smallpox epidemic. There were no cures as such.'

MG

'Most of the 'killers' you describe have been banished from industrialised countries and indeed from most of the developing world. For my journey I had been inoculated against them. The idea is that you are injected with a small amount of the virus, which your immune system then destroys. This defence is then triggered should the actual virus come along, and it is ready to counteract it more effectively. You become, in effect, immune to the disease.

'Furthermore, medicine has advanced so much that major organs, including the heart, are being transplanted from dead donors to those in dire need of replacements.'

TD

'People must live much longer then?'

MG

'This is true, but this has caused the world population to grow rapidly, and people are living longer anyway. This has put great pressure on the social services in developed countries. We do still have deadly diseases, which are incurable – cancer, AIDS, influenza and heart disease to name a few. Not so serious, but still persistent, is the common cold.'

TD

'Overall it seems a much better world for more people than in my day?'

MG

'I think it is Tom, but I am talking about industrialised countries only here. We do not have catastrophic world wars now. True we still have wars as such, but they have tended to be regional in nature. Technology has played a big part in this.'

TD

'Is the world safer then? And what do you mean by technology playing a role?'

MG

'Yes and no. A new source of power has been developed which, when properly handled, can provide 'clean energy', unlike coal! It is called nuclear power. Unfortunately this energy, when harnessed to produce nuclear arms has the ability to destroy the entire planet. Fortunately the nations which have such technology are few and they have no intention of using their nuclear arms.'

TD

'That is very scary. I hope it never happens – no-one would win. I thought the Great War was horrendous enough.'

MG

'Talking of Europe, much has changed since your time. We now have the European Union, which is based mainly on economic co-operation between member states. This has made thoughts of war unthinkable. Even at the time of writing we are headed towards a single European currency called the Euro and Scotland now has a separate parliament from the rest of the UK. Scotch has also changed'

TD

'Scotch whisky changed? How? Impossible!'

MG

'Pioneers like yourself got Scotch accepted as a universal drink in the world markets, and these are still immensely important. Without those sales of high quality blended whisky, the Scotch whisky industry would flounder. Over recent years however, the world has discovered a taste for single malt Scotch whisky and this is growing. Your whisky – Dewars, is still the number one blended Scotch in the USA. I saw it everywhere I travelled from Hawaii to Fiji to Shanghai.'

TD

'I'll drink to that.'

MG

'So will I. Thank you Tom for the inspiration'

TD

'It's my pleasure dear boy. I wonder if someone else will follow in our footsteps a hundred years from now?

MG

'I bet it will be a woman! By the way Tom, our road systems are still named after your horses. They are called dual carriageways.'

TD

'Well the old horse and carriage may have been slow but we got there in the end.'

MG

'Not much has changed then Tom – you can still skirt around London at five miles per hour on a motorway called the M25!'

TD

'Ah well. But before we part Malcolm, tell me…is Scotch still the world's favourite spirit?'

MG

'Absolutely, Tom. You can get it in every country in the world…and I should know! Good-bye Tom. It was a pleasure following in your footsteps.'

TD

'The pleasure was all mine. Good-bye Malcolm.'

APPENDIX

FAMOUS 'DEWARISMS'

'Blessed is the advertising agent who can make two
ideas grow where there was only one before.'

'We have a great regard for old age when it is bottled.'

'If we are to help others, I often wonder
what the others are here for.'

'Keep advertising and advertising will keep you.'

'We see more and more of women each year.'

'Advertising is to business what imagination is to poetry.'

'Respectability is the state of never being caught
doing anything which gives you pleasure.'

'Two is company, three is a corporation.'

'Poets are born and not paid.'

'A philosopher is a man who can look at an
empty glass with a smile.'

'We should not say, "how's business",
but "where is business".'

'Our slogan has always been: "England for Englishmen to live in,
Scotland for Scotsmen to live out of".'

'Minds are like parachutes, they only
function when they open.'

'If you do not advertise you fossilise.'

'Today women display more backbone than men.'

'Some people are always looking for
new kinds of mistakes to make.'

'Experience is merely a matter of buying your
experience cheap and selling it at a profit.'

'Experience is what you get when you are
looking for something else.'

'The beauty specialist said his job
was to make up jokes.'

'Fish stimulates the brain, but fishing
stimulates the imagination.'

'If a man upon his trade relies he must
be either bust or advertise.'

'Never invest in a going concern until you
know which way it is going.'

'The greatest mistake you can make in this life
is to be continually fearing you will make one.'

'Ability without enthusiasm is like
a rifle without a bullet.'

'A teetotaller is one who suffers from
thirst instead of enjoying it.'

'There is no fun like work.'

PERSONAL NOTES

One hundred years ago Johnstons of Elgin were already a long established company and James Johnston, pictured below, will have experienced his fair share of whisky salesmen. They'll have had plenty to discuss over their drams as Johnstons use the same soft highland water in the manufacturing and finishing of their fine cashmere and lambswool cloths, as is used to distil Scotland's finest malt whiskies.

Today Johnstons of Elgin manufacture a luxury range of high quality cashmere and lambswool knitwear, cloths and accessories sold all over the world.

Johnstons *of Elgin*

Newmill Elgin Morayshire IV30 4AF
telephone 01343 554000 facsimile 01343 554055
website www.johnstons-of-elgin.com/.

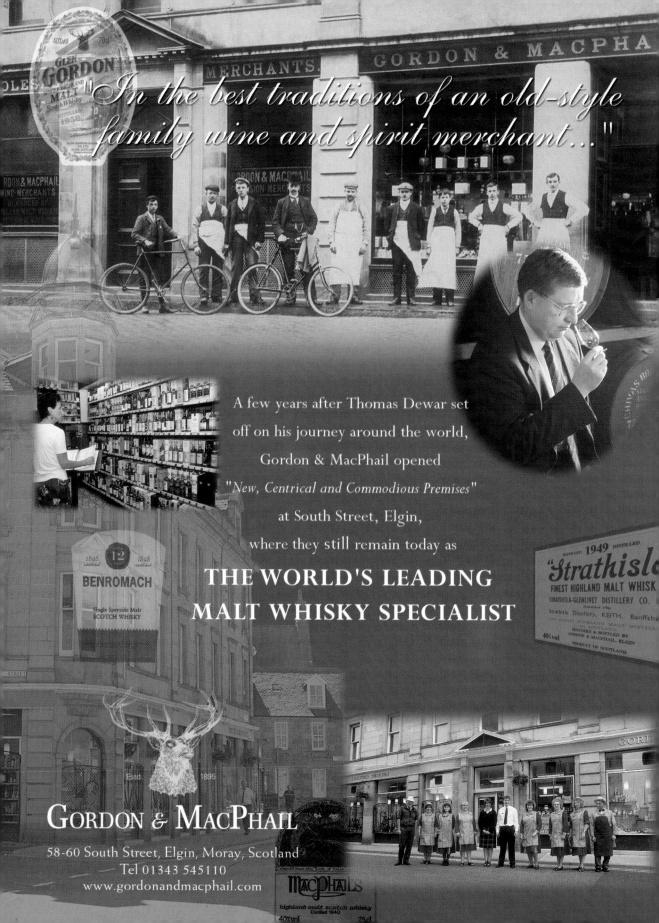

"In the best traditions of an old-style family wine and spirit merchant..."

A few years after Thomas Dewar set off on his journey around the world, Gordon & MacPhail opened "New, Centrical and Commodious Premises" at South Street, Elgin, where they still remain today as

THE WORLD'S LEADING MALT WHISKY SPECIALIST

GORDON & MACPHAIL

58-60 South Street, Elgin, Moray, Scotland
Tel 01343 545110
www.gordonandmacphail.com

PRODUCT OF SCOTLAND

Walkers

·—· ESTABLISHED 1898 ·—·

One hundred years ago

a young Speyside baker,

Joseph Walker, had an

ambition to produce the finest

shortbread in the world.

JOSEPH. WALKER.

1898

HIGHLAND SPRING

- Scottish Natural Mineral Water
- Eau Minéral Naturelle Ecossaise
- Agua Mineral Natural Escocesa
- Agua Mineral Da Escocia

One of the finest Mineral Waters in the world, now exported to over 40 countries worldwide. Direct from our source in Blackford, Scotland.

Export enquiries to:
Highland Spring Ltd,
1 Victoria Square, Victoria Street, St Albans,
Hertfordshire, AL1 3YW, England
Tel: (0044) 01727 843 433
Fax: (0044) 01727 845 059
Email: 106111.1456@compuserve.com

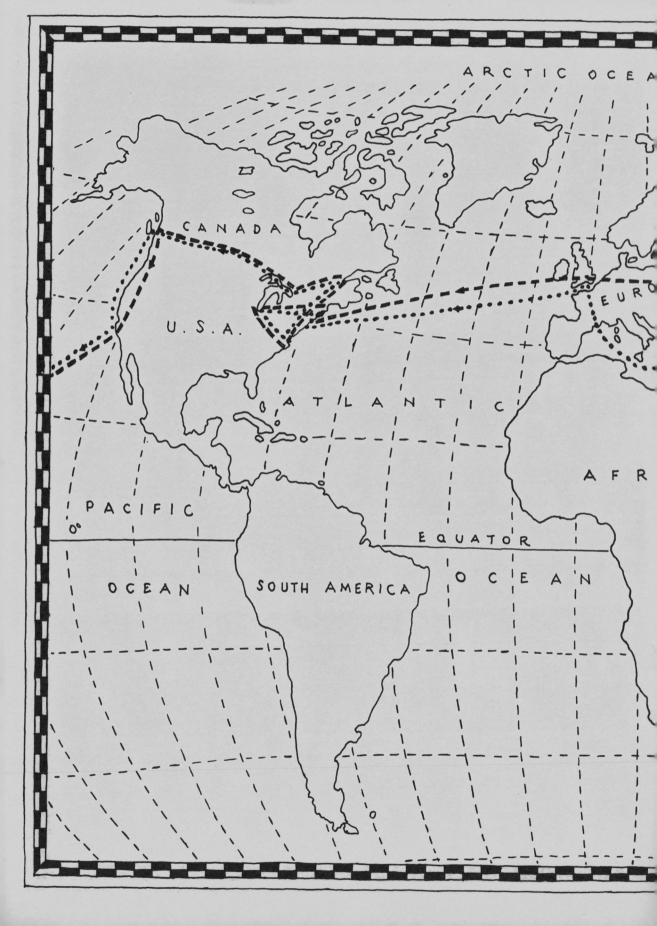